Innovation in the Social Economy

Emerging Best Practice in Ireland and Wales

Edited by
Deiric Ó Broin and Mary Hyland

GLASNEVIN
PUBLISHING

Published in 2014 by

Glasnevin Publishing
2nd Floor, 13 Upper Baggot Street
Dublin 4, Ireland
www.glasnevinpublishing.com

A Catalogue record for this book can be obtained from the British Library.

Papers used by Glasnevin Publishing are from well managed forests and other responsible sources.

ISBN: 978-1-908689-27-6

Publication of this book has been kindly supported by:

CONTENTS

LIST OF FIGURES

LIST OF TABLES

ACKNOWLEDGEMENTS

This book is the result of our discussions and contacts with many people at various places over the course of the past two years. The editors would like to thank the members of the Menter Iontach Nua Steering Committee (Ireland and Wales), DCU Ryan Academy for Entrepreneurship, DCU Business School and Dr. Emer Ní Bhrádaigh (DCU Social Enterprise Champion) for their support, advice and intellectual stimulation. Particular thanks is paid to Liann Buckley and Aifric O'Malley, the Menter Iontach Nua project managers for supporting this book from rough idea to publication and launch.

Deiric Ó Broin would also like to thank the students (past and present) of DCU who engage with so many of the ideas contained in the book and colleagues at the Irish Social Enterprise Network. A special debt of gratitude to the women in my life, my late mother who encouraged me to continue my education, Kathleen who put up with many late night proofing and editing sessions, our daughter Sarah who, in her own unassuming way, persuaded me to complete the project so she could watch Elmo on the laptop.

Mary Hyland would like to thank Natalja Matease for all the tech support along the way and Ronaldo Munck for his advice and support.

Special thanks to the participants on the MSc in Management (Innovation in Social Enterprise). We would both like to acknowledge the contributions made by the participants. These were often challenging but always helpful.

Finally we would like to thank Dr. Helen McGrath of Glasnevin Publishing for her patience and guidance. There would not be a book without it.

CONTRIBUTORS

Sandra Ackers has worked in various accounting roles since 1986, first gaining experience of finance in the private sector with an international oil and gas company and then in 1996 transferring into the third sector to work for one of Wales' leading drug and alcohol charities, which supports individuals coping with substance misuse issues as well as mental health and PTSD problems. Having qualified as a Chartered Management Accountant, Sandra currently manages the charity's finance function and its social enterprise catering businesses. This involved project managing the renovation of a Grade II Listed Building and then setting up a bistro in 2013. Sandra is a recent graduate of the MSc in Management (Innovation in Social Enterprise) from DCU.

Alan Breathnach is the manager of the National Learning Network in County Meath. He is a graduate of the Dublin City University Business School where he completed a Bachelor of Business Studies degree. He has over 10 years experience in community economic development, social enterprise, social inclusion and education provision in a variety of settings. Alan is a recent graduate of the MSc in Management (Innovation in Social Enterprise) from DCU.

Liann Buckley has an undergraduate degree in Social Science from UCC and has completed a MSc in Local and Community Development at DIT. As part of her MSc she completed a thesis on social enterprise and now works as a Social Enterprise Manager for the DCU Ryan Academy. To date this role involved working on the design, delivery and management of Ireland's first online MSc in Social Enterprise and a suite of non-accredited programmes for the sector.

Victoria Burrows is a charity fundraiser and freelance consultant. Victoria has worked in the public and third sectors for 14 years. Roles have included community engagement and communication, funding, grant management and children and young peoples' service development. A strong advocate for safety of children and young people Victoria's most recent role has seen the transition of a regional charity into a vibrant enterprise. She is a recent graduate of the MSc in Management (Innovation in Social Enterprise) from DCU.

Seamus Carlin is a Chartered Marketer by profession with research, analysis and evaluation experience specialising in social impact, social responsibility, social investment and social entrepreneurship. In addition, he has professional practice in the fields of disability, learning disabilities, older people, youth, community development, mental health and sport. He has worked with clients across public, private, philanthropy and third sectors across the UK and Ireland. He is a certified Social Return On Investment practitioner and is a member of the Social Impact Analysts Association and Institute of Management Consultants and Advisers in Ireland. He holds primary and postgraduate degrees in marketing, a MSc in Executive Leadership from the University of Ulster and Boston College, and Seamus is a recent graduate of the MSc in Management (Innovation in Social Enterprise) from DCU.

Margaret Cleary is an experienced community development practitioner and social enterprise manager. Margaret has spent a considerable proportion of her career in Zimbabwe, Tanzania and Uganda where she honed her skills as a strong advocate of sustainable communities. In addition she has worked and volunteered with organisations such as Teach Dara, CAMARA and Amnesty International. She holds degrees in Community Development, Human Rights and Political Science and she is a recent graduate of the MSc in Management (Innovation in Social Enterprise) from Dublin City University. Margaret hopes to continue her work in fostering innovative ideas to create successful enduring social enterprises into the future.

Nóirín Coghlan is currently employed as Community and Family Programme Manager with the Ballymun Whitehall Area Partnership (BWAP) in Dublin. Nóirín has a first class BA (Hons) in Community and Family Studies from NUI, Galway (2010) and is a recent graduate of the MSc in Management (Innovation in Social Enterprise) from DCU. Her career in early childhood care and education spans over thirty years and includes working as a Montessori teacher in Ireland and Canada; with Barnardos Traveller Education Project; and Childcare Coordinator with BWAP. Noirin established The Ballymun Childcare Providers Network in 2005, and is a founding member and director of Start Strong, the children's early care and education advocacy initiative.

She chaired The Balance Matters Programme, an inter-agency collaboration which received a Biomnis Healthcare Innovation award in 2011. She is committed to advancing high quality care and education as a right for all young children in Ireland and chairs the Poppintree Early Education Centre.

Alan Curtis has over 20 years experience in community development, social enterprise and social innovation. Previously employed at managerial level throughout Ireland within the local development and social economy sector Alan now works for Pobal who manage a number of community and social enterprise programmes on behalf of the Irish Government. He is currently team leader for employment activation programmes with the community services and support directorate. Alan holds a MBS (Co-operatives and Social Enterprise) from UCC and a MSc from DCU in Management (Innovation in Social Enterprise).

Michelle Daly-Hayes is the Development Manager at Mid West Spina Bifida and Hydrocephalus Association. Prior to this she worked in the area of corporate communications and digital media. She was elected National President of Junior Chamber International (Ireland) in 2012. Michelle volunteers her time to a number of causes, including being a member of the board of directors of the Blue Box Creative Learning Centre in Limerick. Michelle holds a BA (Politics and Sociology) from the University of Limerick. She is also a recent graduate of the MSc in Management (Innovation in Social Enterprise) from DCU.

Gerry Folan is a Senior Executive Officer with Dublin City Council. He has worked in local government for over 38 years, most of that time with the City Council in Planning and Development, Housing, Human Resources, Local Area Management and Regeneration, and Community and Enterprise. He has worked extensively with European networks on urban development issues, social inclusion and integration. In 2007 he initiated the City Council policy response to the impact of new migration in the city, led the development of a strategic framework on integration for the city, and headed up the Office for Integration of Dublin City Council to guide implementation and coordination of integration policy and actions at city level. Since 2011 he has had responsibility for operational management of homeless services for

Dublin City Council as lead agency responding to homelessness in the Dublin Region. He holds a Barrister at Law Degree from the Honorable Society of Kings Inns and is a recent graduate of the MSc in Management (Innovation in Social Enterprise) from DCU.

Guy Hamilton Evans is the Executive Director and Company Secretary of The Care Society, a rural mid-Wales housing and support charity. Using skills gained whilst previously working in both the private and public sector, he has orchestrated the growth of the charity including establishing a trading subsidiary and a portfolio of social enterprise initiatives which complement existing core activities and the social objectives of the organization. He is also a Director of the Welsh charity 'Tir Coed' and Chairperson of its trading subsidiary 'Wise Woods Wales'. 'Wise Woods Wales' works in partnership with Natural Resources Wales to fell, process and manufacture products whilst providing training opportunities and benefitting the woodland environment. Guy holds a BA (Hons) History from Aberystwyth University and is a recent graduate of the MSc in Management (Innovation in Social Enterprise) from Dublin City University. Guy is a member of the Advisory Board of Aberystwyth University's Business School and actively promotes links between the school and SMEs within the rural mid-Wales area.

Bebhinn Hare is a manager with ten years experience in commercial and non-profit environments. Most recently she consulted on the development of a Marketing Strategy for Healthy Food for All, an initiative working to end Food Poverty on the island of Ireland. She is a two-time Vodafone Foundation World of Difference awardee for her work with Care Local's Plate Pals; a volunteer programme providing mealtime companionship for older people living with Alzheimers. She has presented nationally and internationally on Plate Pals, resulting in innovative partnerships with hospitals and nursing homes. Her interest in social enterprise stems from her enthusiasm to use her prior commercial experience to benefit social causes. Leading from her work in gerontology, she has a wider interest in food and food systems, due to a focus on the whole life cycle and social determinants of health. Bebhinn is a recent graduate of the MSc in Management (Innovation in Social Enterprise) from DCU.

Anthony Hearn is a social housing and enterprise professional currently providing specialist business support packages to housing associations and social enterprises in Wales. With extensive experience of managing a diverse range of specialist supported housing services, Anthony has a wealth of knowledge in engaging with hard to reach communities, groups and individuals. In addition he has developed and project managed a range of developments and services from bespoke complex needs support solutions to large scale homeless hostel developments. Always willing to raise to a challenge, Anthony is a recent graduate of the MSc in Management (Innovation in Social Enterprise) from DCU.

Alison Hill has worked in the voluntary sector for over 20 years. Originally training as a teacher (Further Education) she taught at colleges across Greater Manchester. Subsequently, as Chief Officer of Bolton Council for Voluntary Service her role was to provide services, leadership and representation for the voluntary sector in Bolton. For the last 10 years Alison has been Chief Officer of Caia Park Partnership (CPP), a social enterprise based on a large social housing estate in Wrexham. During this time she has led on the development of 7 social enterprises ranging from a day care nursery to Welsh artisan crafts. All of the enterprises generate income or deliver services for CPP. Alison has recently completed a part-time MSc in Management (Innovation in Social Enterprise) with Dublin City University. In addition she has won the Wales Coop Social Enterprise Champion award 2014 recognising her contribution to social enterprise development in Wales.

Mary Hyland is a Senior Researcher in the Office of Civic Engagement at Dublin City University. Her research is in the inter-connected areas of employment, industrial relations and labour migration as well as in public affairs and political communication. Among her most recent publications are *Trade unions and Migration: A Case for New Organisational Approaches* in Schierup, C.U. Munck, R. Likić-Brborić, B. & Neergaard, A. (eds). *Migration, Precarity and Global Governance: Challenges for Labour*, Oxford: Oxford University Press (pending); *Migration, Regional Integration and Social Transformation: a North-South Comparative Approach* (with Ronnie Munck), Global Social Policy Journal, Vol.13, No 3, 2013; She has acted as editor of Translocations, an open access E-journal on migration in Ireland and as an academic editor and indexer for publications from a range of publishers, including Oxford University Press, Palgrave Macmillan and Ashgate. She has recently completed her PhD which examined the response of the Irish trade union movement to contemporary labour migration and its implications for future trade union organisation. She holds a BA in English and History from NUIG and an MA in Political Communications from DCU.

Maighréad Kelly is a Service Manager with Cheshire Ireland Services in Cork. Cheshire Ireland provides a range of support services to people with both physical disabilities and neurological conditions in their homes, in residential centres, in supported accommodation and in standalone respite facilities. She has over twenty years' experience of supporting people with disabilities to overcome barriers that they face on a daily basis. Previously, she has held positions in Brothers of Charity in Waterford, the National Disability Authority and RehabCare. She is a member of both the Institute for Management Consultants and Advisors and the Institute for Managers of Community and Voluntary Organisations in Ireland. Whilst completing the MSc in Management (Innovation in Social Enterprise) from DCU she has completed work for Cork Craft and Design, SECAD and is currently a member of EcCoWell in Cork, which is an integrated approach to deliver better quality of life to citizens in a sustainable way.

Giustina Francesca Mizzoni holds an MSc in Management (Innovation in Social Enterprise) from DCU, an MA in International Politics (Human Rights) from City University London and a BA in History and Politics from UCD. Presently she works with the CoderDojo Foundation whose vision is a world where every child has the opportunity to learn code and be creative in a safe, social environment. The Foundation supports CoderDojo, the global movement of free coding clubs for young people, presently there are 500+ clubs spread across 50 countries. Her role as Development Lead sees her managing relationships with donors and strategic growth partners. An avid technology fan, she managed the Irish operations of Dogpatch Labs, a coworking space for startup technology companies. Previously she has volunteered with the British Red Cross Refugee Services, Ashoka, and Social Entrepreneurs Ireland.

Paul Murgatroyd holds a MSc in Management (Innovation in Social Enterprise) from Dublin City University and a BA in Geography and Economics. He spent ten years in senior management, conducting research and analysis for a national property company. Paul currently works in the field of operations management for a social enterprise / community enterprise centre, with a focus on promoting socio-economic community development in a disadvantaged area. Paul also holds directorships with Blanchardstown Area Partnership, a Local Community Development Company and with Vassin Ltd, a not-for-profit organisation overseeing Community Employment and Full Time Job Initiative schemes in Dublin.

Deiric Ó Broin is the Chairperson of Menter Iontach Nua, an INTERREG-funded learning, networking and support initiative designed to improve the innovation, creativity and entrepreneurial skills of social enterprises in the INTERREG regions of Ireland and Wales, Programme Chairperson of the Graduate Certificate in Innovation in Social Enterprise at Dublin City University Business School and the Academic and Public Policy Adviser to the Irish Social Enterprise Network. He is a graduate of the Dublin Institute of Technology (Business and Legal Studies), the National College of Industrial Relations (Industrial Relations Management), UCC where he obtained a MBS (Social Enterprise), Keele University, where he completed a MA (Research Ethics) and UCD, where he completed a MA (Politics and Economics) and a PhD (Political Theory). He is Chairperson of the founding committee of the Institute of Economic Development (All-Ireland Branch), a member of the Executive Committee of the Regional Studies Association (Irish Branch) and a senior member of the Institute for Managers of Community and Voluntary Organisations in Ireland.

Roy O'Connor is a Chartered Engineer with his primary degree in Civil, Water and Environmental Management Engineering. He is currently working at the design and management of sustainable transportation projects in Dublin City. These include projects to provide improvements for public transport, cycling and pedestrian infrastructures. A recent graduate of the MSc in Management (Innovation in Social Enterprise) programme at DCU, Roy is working to apply these skills at enhancing the effectiveness of how our transportation infrastructure better serves the integration and connectivity of our urban communities. When Roy is not cycling around the city from project to project he can be found pursuing his other interests and activities. These include supporting the Irish Social Enterprise Network and partaking in small community initiatives such a micro farming and beekeeping.

Aifric O'Malley has an undergraduate degree in Environmental Science from TCD and completed an MSc in Sustainable Development at DIT. Aifric now works as a Social Enterprise Manager for the DCU Ryan Academy with a particular interest in environmental businesses. She recently completed a Graduate Certificate in Digital Marketing from DCU Business School to complement her work in the Academy. Her role on the Menter Iontach Nua project involved working on the design, delivery and management of Ireland's first online MSc in Social Enterprise and a suite of non-accredited programmes for the sector.

Breffni O'Rourke has been working in Fingal County Council since 2004; he was recently appointed Chief Officer for the Local Community Development Committee (LCDC), which provides local government with a leading role in economic and local community development. Prior to his current role he was the coordinator for the government RAPID programme in Blanchardstown, west Dublin. He started his career in 1997 as a community development worker with an Irish welfare organisation in London. In 2000 he moved to a Home Office-funded project where he received a commendation from the Metropolitan Police in his role as Race Crime Projects Development Worker. Upon moving to Dublin he was Deputy Manager of the London Borough of Merton's, crime and disorder reduction partnership. Breffni recently completed the MSc in Management (Innovation in Social Enterprise) with Dublin City University.

Eoghan Stack graduated as an Electrical Engineer from University College Cork in 1997 and began his career designing integrated circuits with one of Ireland's most successful R&D teams in 3Com Technologies. In 2005, Eoghan began working with one of Ireland's leading entrepreneurs, Declan Ryan, in Ryan's 10-year limited-life venture philanthropy fund, The One Foundation. Over the lifetime of the fund as Director of Investment Impact, Eoghan worked with over 25 Irish and Vietnamese non-profit companies, leading in over 25 multi-million euro investments and working with senior management teams to improve company effectiveness to deliver significant social impact. In 2013, Eoghan joined Dublin City University's Ryan Academy for Entrepreneurs as Chief Commercial Officer. The academy is a partnership between DCU and the Ryan Family and aims to be the leading supporter of entrepreneurs and innovation in Ireland. Eoghan is Deputy Chair of the Board of Philanthropy Ireland and also serves on the Boards of other non-profit organisations. Eoghan is a recent graduate of the MSc in Management (Innovation in Social Enterprise) with Dublin City University.

Deirdre Whitfield works fulltime with Wicklow County Council in the Community, Culture and Social Development Section. A lifelong commitment to community development and social justice has characterized Deirdre's academic journey. She holds a BA (Hons) in Sociology from the Open University, and has also studied Rural Development and Women's Studies in UCD. Throughout her time in local government, Deirdre has undertaken a number of courses with the IPA to further broaden and strengthen her skills set within this sector. Deirdre is a recent graduate of the MSc in Management (Innovation in Social Enterprise) with Dublin City University.

FOREWORD

The economies of Ireland and Wales have changed significantly since 2008. We have seen the collapse of one model of development and the partial emergence of something different; its outlines are dim but it appears to be substantively different. The social economy and the potential role of social enterprises are rapidly gaining in visibility in debates about the possible nature of this emerging model and I am glad to state that Dublin City University is situated at the centre of such debates.

A key role for DCU is to contribute to, and to shape the ongoing debates between the academy, practitioners and policy makers. As a University of Enterprise, DCU proudly emphasizes its innovative roots and how our origins underpin our mission to translate academic research into practical and grounded contributions.

This mission is perfectly reflected in our involvement in the Menter Iontach Nua MSc initiative for emerging leaders in social enterprise and our ongoing support for, and work with, a wide range of social enterprise-related projects, including DCU's designation as Europe's first AshokaU Changemaker Campus, our pioneering decision to create the position of Social Enterprise Champion to promote social enterprise in the university, our work with the Irish Social Enterprise Network and Social Entrepreneurs Ireland and the ongoing work of many DCU staff on the voluntary boards of local social enterprises and national support organizations. It also reflects our involvement in the President of Ireland's Ethics Initiatives and our focus on rethinking our models of economic development to ensure more equitable outcomes for our citizens.

In this regard, I am delighted with the applied nature and practice-focused contributions from our graduates' contributions to this book. These are a formidable group of mid-career professionals in the social enterprise, social finance, venture philanthropy, local government and local development sectors in Ireland and Wales working together to develop grounded, just and sustainable solutions to many of the challenges facing our local economies.

[signature]

President
Dublin City University

CHAPTER 1
INTRODUCTION

Deiric Ó Broin

Introduction
This book arises from the hard work and commitment of a large number of people who were involved in the Menter Iontach Nua initiative. This includes the students who participated in the MSc in Management (Innovation in Social Enterprise) in Dublin City University Business School, colleagues from the Business School and the DCU Ryan Academy for Entrepreneurship and our partners in Bangor University and Business in the Community Wales. As a group our work was facilitated by funding from the INTERREG 4A Ireland Wales Territorial Co-operation Programme 2007-2013. Without their advice and support there would not have been a Menter Iontach Nua initiative, an MSc programme or a book.

This introductory chapter will outline the origins of the Menter Iontach Nua initiative as it relates to the book, broadly review the contents of the chapters, and finally outline the potential contribution the book can make.

Background to Menter Iontach Nua
Liann Buckley and Aifric O'Malley provide a considered review of the operation of the Menter Iontach Nua initiative in their chapter but the background to the initiative and the process leading up to an agreement between the various parties to make a submission is important. As noted above there are four partners in the initiative, funded by INTERREG 4A.

DCU and the DCU Ryan Academy for Entrepreneurship
DCU is a young, dynamic and ambitious university with a distinctive mission to transform lives and societies through education, research and innovation. Since admitting its first students in 1980, DCU has grown in both student numbers and size and now occupies a 72 acre site in Glasnevin and a related 10 acre Innovation Campus within 10 minutes of the university. It is currently engaged in a process whereby it will incorporate St. Patrick's College, Drumcondra; the Mater Dei Institute of Education; and the Church of Ireland College of Education.

DCU Ryan Academy is a non-profit, joint venture between Dublin City University and the Ryan Family (Ryanair) that aims to be the leading supporter of entrepreneurs and innovation in Ireland. Its vision is one where entrepreneurship and innovation are viewed as key drivers of business success and the DCU Ryan Academy as a catalyst in the development of an entrepreneurial mind-set. Its mission is to stimulate that mind-set and and to promote an innovation focus among Irish SMEs, corporates, start-ups and researchers through a range of training, leadership and funding initiatives. It bridges the gap between academia and entrepreneurial practice through its unique partnership of Ireland's leading young university, Dublin City University, and the family of one of Ireland's best known entrepreneurs, Tony Ryan.

Bangor University
Founded in 1884, Bangor University has a long tradition of excellence both for academic standards and student experience. It has more than 11,000 students and over 650 teaching staff based in 23 Academic Schools grouped into five Colleges. Bangor University's mission is to be a leading research-led university with an international reputation for teaching and research, providing a supportive multicultural environment, promoting widening access and inclusiveness, and supporting the economic, social and cultural well-being of Wales and the wider community it serves.

NorDubCo
NorDubCo was established in 1996 to promote the social, economic and civic development of North Dublin. At the time a very specific set of challenges faced the region and NorDubCo was configured to address those challenges. Since its establishment, it has worked to ensure that sustainable economic, social and civic development takes place in the region. It has worked to create a positive vision for community and working life there, a vision that seeks to embrace all of the region's communities.

BITC Wales
BITC Wales is a unique business-led charity, focused on promoting responsible business. It has an established 25-year track record in Wales and works closely with more than 150 local companies, ranging

from SMEs to large corporates. Its aim is to help Welsh businesses prosper through maximising the commercial benefits of responsible business practice, whilst making a real difference to the people and environment of Wales.

INTERREG 4A

The Ireland Wales Territorial Co-operation Programme 2007-2013 (INTERREG 4A) aims to further develop Irish-Welsh co-operation in the areas of employment, innovation, climate change and sustainable development. INTERREG means 'Inter-regional' which represents the building of links between regions in the European Union. Managed in Ireland by the Southern and Eastern Regional Assembly on behalf of the Irish Government, the Welsh Government and the European Commission, the Programme is part-funded by the European Regional Development Fund (ERDF). It builds on the success of the Ireland Wales INTERREG IIIA Programme (2000-2006) which covered themes of business and rural development, training, ICT, marine environment, culture, heritage and tourism. The Welsh European Funding Office was the lead authority during this Programming period.

The Ireland Wales Programme 2007-13 seeks to further develop the cross-border region by:

- Improving the overall economic, environmental and social well-being of the Ireland Wales co-operation area;
- Achieving a more cohesive, balanced and sustainable development of the area;
- Contributing to the greater competitiveness of the region and that of the EU in a globalised world.

It has an overall aim of addressing issues relating to innovation, entrepreneurship, the knowledge economy, climate change and sustainable development and providing more and better jobs between the two EU neighbours. Menter Iontach Nua was funded under priority 1 theme 2, skills for competitiveness and employment integration.

Building an Inquiring and Collaborative Initiative

The opportunities offered by INTERREG funding encouraged the then potential partners as outlined above, to examine the possibility of a joint project. We learned that though we were culturally similar and shared many perspectives on the world, our countries development

3

trajectories were distinctly different. While there were sufficient similarities to facilitate joint learning, our differences were critical. It was these that held the potential for change. For the purposes of the Menter Iontach Nua initiative we focused on the area of social enterprise. Our Welsh colleagues were interested in the phenomenal success of the Irish credit union movement, the creation of an enterprise culture in many Irish citizens, the role of our larger agricultural co-operatives, how EU funding had aided Ireland's economic development, and finally the lessons we had learned, if any, from the collapse of the Celtic Tiger.

Equally we were curious about their legislative framework for social enterprise, regarded by many to be very facilitative of the establishment and consolidation of social enterprises, the supportive role played by local government with regard to social enterprise, the role of their three government-funded national social enterprise support organisations (there are none in Ireland), and the public policy focus on the re-establishment of mutuals as a vibrant component of the economy.[1] There was no equivalent process of investigation and reflection in Ireland.

Each country offered the other an opportunity to engage, learn, and support the reflective processes being undertaken in each country. Of

---

1 The Welsh Co-operative and Mutuals Commission (WCMC) was established in July 2012 to make recommendations to the Minister for Economy, Science and Transport on growing and developing the co-operative and mutual economy in Wales in order to create jobs and wealth. The Commission's report (2014) sets out its conclusions and recommendations. In the course of its work, the Commission received written and oral evidence from nearly 100 individuals and organisations. It concluded that "conventional approaches to economic growth and development are not sufficient alone to achieve the improvement in the social and economic wellbeing of people in Wales" (2014: 4). The Commission contends that co-operatives and mutuals offer significant economic, social and environmental benefits compared with ordinary businesses and that "Wales needs a step-change in the number, performance and impact of co-operatives, mutuals and other socially-owned businesses if the economy is to be transformed (2014: 4).

As noted earlier there is no direct Irish equivalent. The most relevant recent development is probably the government's decision to request Forfás, the national enterprise and science policy advice and support agency, to review the potential of the social enterprise sector as part of the Action Plan for Jobs 2013. The primary objective of the exercise was to analyse the current performance and potential of the social economy in Ireland to contribute to job creation, growth and economic well-being. There were very significant constraints on the research and the sector was defined in a very narrow way.

course there were little quirks we had to learn about that makes all transnational projects so stimulating. Public discourse in Wales tends to discuss the 2007 crash in terms of the bank crisis in the UK. It was interesting to hear how many commentators in turn linked this to the decisions to demutualise mutuals and building societies like Northern Rock and the Halifax. Vince Cable described this as "one of the great acts of economic vandalism in modern times" (WCMC 2014: 2) and argued that it probably accentuated and deepened the UK's banking crisis. In Ireland we tend to talk about the 2008 crash and link it to the collapse of the property market and the related implosion of our banking sector. Both crises share some similar roots and yet remain distinctively Irish and Welsh. As a result, our reactions and proposed methods of escaping the seemingly unending recessions are different.

Setting the economic and political context

Ó Riain (2014: 4-5) clearly outlines the origins of Ireland's economic crisis. Building on the earlier work of the National Economic and Social Council he details the multifaceted aspect of it. At the core was a financial crisis arising from "an unholy combination of property speculation by developers, reckless lending by banks and a lack of governmental oversight and regulation created a property and banking bubble" (2014: 4). A fiscal crisis arose as the public finances struggled to meet the costs of bailing out the banks and the collapse in property-linked tax revenues. This was reinforced by an economic crisis as competitiveness waned and domestic demand collapsed. The financial, fiscal and economic crises "drove a major social crisis based on negative equity and mortgage arrears, cutbacks in public services and disastrous rises in unemployment" (2014: 5). In turn these created a reputational crisis as international lenders were reluctant to finance government debt. This culminated in an EU-IMF bailout in November 2010. Finally these five crises "hastened and were reinforced by a sixth, broader crisis of political capacity, solidarity and action" (2014: 5.).

From a macro Irish perspective we wanted to learn how to remake our social, economic and political systems to avoid a similar occurrence. How could we develop resilience in our key systems? What could we learn from Welsh social enterprises that could contribute to that objective? What could they learn from us that would allow them to develop the model of development the Welsh government articulated,

"...growing and developing the co-operative and mutual economy in Wales to create jobs and wealth" (WCMC, 2014: 8).

While acknowledging the terrible human costs of the recessions in Ireland and Wales it is important to note how unusual this period is. As Merrett and Walzer note, "we live in paradoxical times" (2004: 3). We have witnessed the dominance of *laissez-faire* policymakers advocating the expansion of global markets through free trade agreements (Cohen 1995) and the financialisation[2] of many economies (Fine *et al.* 2013). Consequently, local producers and workers must increase their efficiency and scale of operations to compete. At the same time many advocates of the market promoted the merits of personal responsibility, community and local control. These conflicting policy prescriptions confront social and economic development practitioners with a "conundrum" (Merrett and Walzer, 2004: 3). How can communities composed of locally-owned businesses, including farms, local public service providers and "place-bound consumers" (2004: 3) compete against intense global economic pressures that undermine the social and civic relations that many take for granted? As we emerge, slowly for many, from the recent crisis we have had an opportunity to reflect on how we move forward, what do we rebuild, where do we start from, how should the market, state and society interact?

From an Irish perspective the President of Ireland's Ethics Initiative has been to the forefront in recognising this opportunity to meaningfully reflect on our model of development. In his inaugural address President Higgins stated:

I also intend to hold a number of Presidency Seminars which may reflect and explore themes important to our shared life yet separate and wider than legislative demand, themes such as the restoration of

---

[2] Financialisation is a relatively new term and has its roots primarily in heterodox economics and Marxist political economy (Fine 2007: 2-4) although it is increasingly adopted by orthodox economists. It has also been understood in a number of different ways. First, at the most casual level, it refers to the expansion and proliferation of financial markets over the past thirty years, during which the ratio of global financial assets to global GDP has risen three times, from 1.5 to 4.5 (Palma, 2009). Second, financialisation has been associated with the expansion of speculative assets at the expense of mobilising and allocating investment for real activity. Third, this is because financialisation has been understood as both the expansion and the proliferation of financial instruments and services. These have given birth to a whole range of financial institutions and markets, e.g. sub-prime mortgages. Fourth, at a systemic level, financialisation has been located in terms of the dominance of finance over industry.

trust in our institutions, the ethical connection between our economy and society, the future of a Europe built on peace, social solidarity and sustainability (2011).

This book can be situated in this context. It is the product of a reflective process, moderated in part by academics, but driven and shaped by the participants on the programme. The Menter Iontach Nua initiative gave its participants time, support and an opportunity to reflect on their roles so that they might, in future, engage with their organisations and develop new approaches to shared problems.

Themes

This book draws together contributions from practitioners in the social enterprise, social finance, venture philanthropy, local government and local development sectors in both countries. It considers the impact of innovation on the social economy and explores its capacity to contribute to both the Irish and Welsh economies as they begin to recover from the global crisis. In reflecting this aim, the book examines aspects of public policy, in particular, economic development, labour market, housing, childcare, health, the economic development drivers of public infrastructure investment, and national social enterprise support infrastructure. It also examines a range of social enterprise-centric areas, including, marketing and branding, leadership, sectoral representation and approaches to financial sustainability.

With regard to the interaction between the various areas of public policy, the chapters address very different processes yet there are recurring themes. For example, there is a troubling lack of evidence-based policy in many areas while the highly isolated nature of policy-making processes also pervades many of the policy areas addressed.

In Chapter, 2, Ó Broin situates the debate about the social economy in the context of the recent collapse of Ireland's neo-corporatist social partnership model and the multifaceted crises facing Ireland. In particular, the chapter examines the public policy supports and the constraints arising in the ongoing programme of austerity. In doing so it reviews public discourse regarding appropriate models of sustainable economic development and the consequences for public policy formulation. The chapter contends that the prospect of public policy facilitating the expansion of the social economy in Ireland remains a distinct possibility.

The importance of capacity building is addressed in a number of chapters. In Chapter 3 Buckley and O'Malley focus on the role of higher education institutions. What emerges clearly is that many of the key successes of the Menter Iontach Nua initiative, including, its ability to: nurture future leaders in the sector; facilitate networking and peer learning between social enterprises in Ireland and Wales; and build capacity in smaller social enterprises or start-ups, reflect an unmet need in the sector and its as yet untapped potential.

Chapter 4, on the social enterprise sector's efforts to collectively organise, also of necessity addresses the issue of capacity building. As Hare, Mizzoni, O'Connor, O'Rourke and Stack show, the sector displays significant potential but it is vital that, collectively, it takes the appropriate steps to ensure its views are appropriately articulated. Chapter 5 further develops this theme. Carlin, Murgatroyd, Coghlan and Breathnach specifically examine the area of capacity building for social enterprises in marginalised communities. Their case study of Innovate Ballymun reflects the grounded nature of their analysis. As a group of professionals working in the sector, their chapter teases out the complex and interrelated operational and policy challenges facing childcare social enterprises operating in marginalised communities. The chapter concludes that it is critical to develop a focus on evidence-based practice to support policymakers and social enterprises to make better-informed decisions in order to achieve higher quality outcomes and impacts for all children, especially those in disadvantaged areas. They recommend that social enterprises adopt a financial sustainability approach detailed in the chapter and use the toolkit proposed and the resources at their disposal to meet their mission and sustain their work in the longer-term.

Continuing the practical and experience-based approach to emerging best practices in social enterprises in both countries, Chapter 6, Chapter 7 and Chapter 8 detail the authors' involvement in projects that challenge the existing understanding of effective service delivery. In Chapter 6, Ackers, Burrows, Hamilton Evans and Hearn outline their involvement in a social enterprise proposal to provide services to a group of ex-offender military veterans in Wales. The chapter demonstrates that the model outlined could meet the challenges which have arisen from the changes to the offender management process and the move towards wider community integration. In addition it supports a variety of related positive outcomes, including community food growing, ex-offender physical and mental wellbeing and reductions in reoffending.

In Chapter 7, Curtis, Whitfield, Cleary and Folan propose a new model of social enterprise housing to address key aspects of the current housing shortage, while facilitating additional investment. Their conclusions suggest that the key success factor will be an integrated public policy approach at both national and local level with, in particular, the Department of Environment, Community and Local Government and the recently established Local Community Development Committees operating at city and county level.

Maighréad Kelly's chapter demonstrates that social enterprises designed specifically to support people with intellectual disabilities have greater potential to support those employees to overcome the barriers to employment. The chapter also warns of the dangers of establishing social enterprises which are nothing more than a modern version of the segregated sector of sheltered workshops and job enclaves.

The final two chapters of the book review current academic research on entrepreneurship and marketing for social enterprises. In Chapter 9, Daly-Hayes considers current approaches to analysing entrepreneurial characteristics and provides a comparative analysis of family business entrepreneurs and social entrepreneurs.

She suggests that social entrepreneurs and family business entrepreneurs share common characteristics but differ in their motivations and applications, i.e. they share essential 'entrepreneurial DNA' but the output of their work is different and benefits different groups. In addition the chapter finds that a significant percentage of social entrepreneurs evolve in an organic sense from a family business entrepreneurial background. Linking to the earlier theme of capacity building, the chapter suggests that a better understanding of these traits and the identification of definite links between the two types of entrepreneur in Ireland will contribute to more effective training and development support.

In Chapter 10 Hill examines the area of marketing and, in particular, the concept of brand personality. The chapter notes that while there is a paucity of literature relating to brand personality in social enterprises specifically, it is possible to draw on the literature that evidences the commercial value of brand personality in the for-profit sector and the important role brand personality plays in communicating values and attracting donations in the non-profit sector. The chapter contends that, as a hybrid of those two sectors, social enterprises could benefit from the positive impacts brand personality brings to both camps.

The chapters in this book explore the social economy and social enterprises from a variety of perspectives. What binds them is their acknowledgement of the importance of both and the requirement to recognise their diverse roles in addressing the needs of local communities. The book presents the argument for more considered engagement by government with the potential of the social economy and points to the significant role it has played in other EU member states which could be replicated in Ireland and Wales.

By seeking to highlight how, for example, governments need to develop an understanding that the social economy is more than an adjunct to the state and market and by examining the need for an effective enabling environment for the social economy in Ireland and Wales, this book emphasises that the social economy has the potential to be a vital component of contemporary society. Recognising this is the first step towards ensuring that the social economy is able to fulfil its potential – a potential with profound implications for the communities in which we live.

CHAPTER 2
BUILDING INCLUSIVE ECONOMIES: THE SOCIAL ECONOMY AND PUBLIC POLICY OPTIONS IN AN ERA OF AUSTERITY

Deiric Ó Broin

Introduction

This chapter situates the debate about the social economy in the context of the recent collapse of Ireland's neo-corporatist social partnership model and the ongoing economic crises facing Ireland.[3] In doing so it examines the paucity of robust public discourse regarding appropriate models of sustainable economic development and the consequences for public policy formulation. It also reviews two distinct rationales for developing the social economy, development and instrumental, through the work of Erik Olin Wright and Elinor Ostrom. The chapter concludes with broad recommendations for policy makers and stakeholders in the social economy.

The Irish case is pertinent for those involved in the public policy debate on the social economy internationally for a number of reasons. Despite the resilience of many of the institutions of social partnership to previous upheavals the scale and the multi-stranded nature of the current crises have been fatal (Ó Broin 2009). Some of the outlines of a new model of public deliberation and economic governance exist but there remains a great deal of 'institutional space' in which to innovate.[4] It is this 'institutional space', the extremely fluid nature of political opinion and the constraints arising from the economic austerity programme agreed with the EU/ECB/IMF, that give added relevance to the Irish experience. For example, the proposed expansion of the delivery of existing public services by locally-accountable social

---

[3] As noted earlier the book uses the term 'crises' rather than 'crisis' because of the multi-stranded and separate nature of the economic, political and regulatory challenges facing Ireland.

[4] These include the changes at national level like the establishment of the Irish Fiscal Advisory Council, the Government's Economic Management Council, and changes at local level which include a series of councillor-centred reforms of the Irish local government and local development systems and establishment of a more coherent and structured enterprise system linked to a reformed local government systems. One could also include a new openness to social enterprises playing an enhanced role in local economies.

enterprises, using public procurement as a tool to enhance local economies (Doyle and Lalor 2010) has much to recommend it but doesn't appear to be a realistic component of the ongoing public sector reform process.

Discussing the Social Economy and Social Enterprise

The OECD observes that across the EU "the social economy, whilst in no way a new phenomenon, has been reinvigorated in recent decades" (2007: 9). This new vibrancy is linked to the "constant and seemingly ever growing pressure" on the welfare state in Europe "to justify its very existence" (Hay and Wincott, 2012: 1). While the pressure on the welfare state has been an important trigger in stimulating the growth and development of the social economy, other factors, including changes to local economies, the exclusion of some vulnerable groups and a gradual move away from traditional conceptions of civil society organisations towards more dynamic, issue-oriented organisations, have also contributed to the reinvigoration of the sector. Social enterprises have:

> moved to fill the gaps left by the market and the state, and have shown themselves to be innovative, adaptable and responsive to local needs when provided with the opportunity and environment which enables them to fill their potential (OECD, 2007: 9).

Exploring issues such as the role of the social economy in service provision and the contribution it can make to local development and examining how a supportive and enabling environment can be created for the social economy and social enterprises, this chapter, and others in the book, highlight the fundamental role of the social economy in improving the lives of, not only, society's most vulnerable, but also communities as a whole. The challenge is to ensure that the social economy is able to play that role to best effect.

What is the Social Economy? What is a Social Enterprise?

Given its critical role, it is clearly important to develop a clear understanding of what the social economy is. However, defining it is not without difficulty. Attempts to define it have drawn on two main approaches. The first seeks to identify those legal and institutional forms which are part of the social economy, namely associations, mutual benefit societies and co-operatives. The second focuses on the common principles which inform those organisations, notably the primacy of individuals and communities over profit, although without completely limiting the distribution of profit (as the US non-profit approach does).

It is important to note, and this is repeated through many chapters of the book, that there is, as of yet, no uniform language and understanding around the idea of social enterprise. Many definitions exist and a wide variety of organisational forms are adopted by social enterprises around the world. For example, while the definitions adopted by Forfás, the Irish Social Enterprise Network, Social Enterprise UK, Scottish Social Enterprise and the Social Enterprise Alliance in the United States share key components, they are distinct from one another.

The OECD defines social enterprise as:

> …any private activity conducted in the public interest, organised with an entrepreneurial strategy, but whose main purpose is not the maximisation of profit but the attainment of certain economic and social goals, and which has the capacity for bringing innovative solutions to the problems of social exclusion and unemployment (OECD, 1999: 1).

More recently, the European Commission has defined a social enterprise as being:

> … an operator in the social economy whose main objective is to have a social impact rather than make a profit for its owners or shareholders. It operates by providing goods and services for the market in an entrepreneurial and innovative fashion and uses its profits primarily to achieve social objectives. It is managed in an open and responsible manner and, in particular, involves employees, consumers and stakeholders affected by its commercial activities (European Commission, 2011: 4).

The different definitions of social enterprise underline different aspects of the same reality. In Europe, social enterprises are closely linked to, and emanate from, the tradition of the social economy, which is characterised by principles and values such as solidarity, the primacy of people over capital, and democratic and participative governance. In Europe, the social economy gathers entities such as co-operatives, associations, mutuals and foundations.

Social enterprises take various legal forms in different countries across Europe. These forms include solidarity enterprises; co-operatives or limited liability social co-operatives; collective interest co-operatives, as have been adopted in Italy, France, Spain, Portugal and Greece; social purpose or collective interest companies in Belgium; and community interest companies in the United Kingdom. A review of the legal structures and legislation in a number of European countries that have adopted national laws regulating social enterprises (i.e. Belgium, Finland, France, Italy, Poland, Portugal and the United Kingdom) reveals that these laws address common issues including the definition of social enterprise; asset allocation; stakeholder and governance systems; and accountability and responsibility towards internal and external stakeholders. These "national laws provide different legal solutions based on specific cultural contexts" (OECD, 2013: 3).

For the purposes of this book we contend that what is critical about the idea of the social economy is that it seeks to capture both the social element and the economic element, inherent in those organisations which inhabit the space between the market and the state. It is important to recognise that not all social economy organisations are focused on economic activity. Indeed the social economy includes advocacy organisations and also those, such as foundations, who redistribute resources. However, the term is a useful one because of its inclusiveness, and ability to incorporate new organisational forms which have emerged, such as social enterprises.

Cause for hope?
In Ireland there exist the components of a potentially robust and facilitative support framework:
- Ireland has the highest per-capita credit union membership in the world;
- Historically Irish civil society has supported the establishment of human-centred economic and social institutions and activities (Ó Broin and Kirby 2009);
- There is significant philanthropic support for social economy-

linked organisations;[5]
- It retains an extensive nationwide network of rural agri-business and community service co-operatives;[6]
- The state funds a very significant social enterprise support programme, one of the largest in the European Union;[7]
- National civil society representative organisations are actively calling for the development of a more supportive public policy framework to expand the social economy.

Despite the above the social economy is widely accepted to be underdeveloped in Ireland, representing only 3% of GDP compared to 4%-7% in other EU member states (SEETF 2012). In addition Irish public policy retains a very strong and distinct pro-private enterprise bias (Kirby 2010) and calls for support for the social economy are often perceived as attempts to undermine private enterprise and the role of the market. In addition Irish public policy efforts in this area tend to use the market-oriented discourse of 'social entrepreneurship' rather than the more society-oriented discourse of 'social economy' (Ó Broin 2012). As the situation evolves a variety of social, economic, civic, governmental and political processes and issues will impact key decisions. These include:
- The strong desire on the part of civil society to establish a robust social economy component of the national economy;
- The openly pro-market bias of many Irish government agencies;
- The economic, financial and policy constraints imposed as a result of the austerity programme;
- The highly open nature of the Irish economy, one of the most globalised in the world;
- The advocacy actions of existing social economy actors;
- The outcome of debates between proponents of social entrepreneurship and social economy;
- The establishment of appropriate national social economy support agencies;

---

[5] See http://socialentrepreneurs.ie/, http://www.ageingwellnetwork.com/ and http://www.guinness.com/en-ie/arthursday/fund.html for more details.
[6] See http://www.forfas.ie/publication/search.jsp?ft=/publications/2007/Title,706,en.php for more details.
[7] See https://www.pobal.ie/FundingProgrammes/CommunityServicesProgramme/Pages/CSP%20Home.aspx for more details.

- The implementation of a radical local government reform process which includes a proposed social economy support function;[8]
- The political decisions taken by the two current government parties.

Analytical Framework

This chapter uses the frameworks developed by Erik Olin Wright (2013) and Elinor Ostrom (1999) to examine the potential for the development of social economies. The frameworks are very different in perspective but provide a powerful conceptualisation of the developmental potential offered by the social economy and the instrumental effectiveness offered by reordering many economic activities to improve their impact.

In relation to the social economy Wright's key argument is that the development of the social economy can constitute an interstitial transformation, i.e.

> ... *new forms of social empowerment in capitalist society's niches and margins, often where they do not seem to pose any immediate threat to dominant classes and elites* (2013: 20).

The central theoretical idea is that building alternatives on the ground in whatever spaces are possible both serves a critical ideological function by showing that alternative ways of working and living are possible, and "potentially erodes constraints on the spaces themselves" (Wright, 2013: 20).[9] Wright (2010) suggests that the social economy may

---

[8] See http://www.environ.ie/en/PublicationsDocuments/FileDownLoad,31310,en.pdf for more details.

[9] Wright (2013: 17-18) uses the term 'social economy' to "designate configurations of social empowerment within an economy in which the state is not involved". He outlines three separate configurations: (a) Social Capitalism, (b) the Core Social Economy and (c) the Co-operative Market Economy. The term social capitalism is used to describe a power configuration in which secondary associations of civil society, through a variety of mechanisms, directly affect the way economic power is used. The core social economy goes beyond social capitalism by constituting an alternative way of directly organizing economic activity that is distinct from capitalist market production, state organized production, and household production. Wrights suggests that Wikipedia is a "striking example of core social economy". It produces knowledge and disseminates information outside of markets and without state support. Its funding is provided by donations from participants and supporters. In a cooperative market economy, all workers jointly control the economic power represented by the capital in the firm. If individual cooperative firms

also be conceived as a "real utopia" since it presents a plausible vision of a radical alternative and a project of emancipatory social change:

> *The 'social economy' constitutes an alternative way of directly organizing economic activity that is distinct from capitalist market production, state organized production, and household production. Its hallmark is the production organized by collectivities directly to satisfy human needs not subject to the discipline of profit-maximization or state-technocratic rationality* (Wright 2010:140–141).

The concept of "co-production" was originally developed by Elinor Ostrom at Indiana University during the 1970s to describe and delimit the involvement of ordinary citizens in the production of public services. As a result, the term "co-production" is used to describe the potential relationship that could exist between the "regular producer" (street-level police officers, schoolteachers, or health workers) and their clients who want to be transformed by the service into safer, better-educated or healthier persons.

Initially co-production had a clear focus on the role of individuals or groups of citizens in the production of public services. Co-production is, therefore, defined by the mix of activities that both public service providers and citizens contribute to the provision of public services. The former are involved as professionals or 'regular producers', while 'citizen production' is based on voluntary efforts of individuals or groups to enhance the quality and/or quantity of services they receive.

Within European discourse, co-production tends to refer to the growing direct and organized involvement of citizens in the production of their own social services (Pestoff, 2012: 1106). For example, parents participate in the co-production of their own childcare, both individually and collectively by joining a parent association or co-operative preschool that produces such services in France, Germany and Sweden. We also find ample evidence of co-management and co-governance of childcare services in some European countries.

---

join together in a larger association, collectively providing finance, training, and other kinds of support, they begin to transcend the capitalist character of their economic environment by constituting a cooperative market economy. The Mondragon Cooperative Corporation is an example.

In her seminal article on co-production, "Crossing the Great Divide" (1999), Ostrom compares the conditions for co-production in two developing countries, i.e., in water systems in suburban areas in Brazil[10] and elementary education in rural Nigeria. In the latter she notes that villagers were traditionally engaged in several community projects, including building roads and the maintenance of school buildings. However, she notes the detrimental effects of centralisation and frequent changes in government policy on primary education. She compared four Nigerian villages, two where parents valued education highly and focused on primary education, with good results in terms of pupils passing their school exams (85 per cent). In two other villages parents valued education less and contributed very little to the local primary schools. Without parental support the teachers were incapacitated and demoralized and the children only obtained a scattered education, if at all. She concludes that when co-production is discouraged by the government taking over schools that villagers had perceived as their own, by creating chaotic changes in who is responsible for financing them and by top-down command administration, etc., only the most determined citizens will persist in co-production activities (1999).

When exploring citizen involvement in the co-production of social services in Europe, we need to consider two-related issues: the ease of involvement and the motivation of individuals to participate in the co-production of social services. How easy is it for citizens to become involved in the provision of social services and why do they become active participants in the service provision process? The ease or facility of citizens becoming involved will depend on several things, like the distance to the service provider, the information available to citizens

---

[10] Condominial sewerage is the term used to describe the application of simplified sewerage coupled with consultations and ongoing interactions between users and agencies during planning and implementation. The term is used primarily in Latin America, particularly in Brazil, and is derived from the term *condominio*, which means housing block. From an engineering perspective there is no difference between designing a regular sewage system and a condominial one. However, bureaucratically a condominially-designed system includes the participation of the individuals and owners who will be served and can often result in lower costs due to shorter runs of piping. This is achieved by local concentration of sewage from a single "housing block". Thus a number of dwellings are grouped into a "block" known as a condominium. The condominium may share no other aspects of ownership or relation except geographic proximity. In addition, individuals and owners may share a role in the maintenance of the sewers at the block level.

about the service and its provision, etc. They are related to the time and effort required for citizens to become involved and might therefore be seen as the transaction costs of participation. If, and when, opportunities exist for motivated citizens to participate actively in the co-production of a social service, lowering the transaction costs will make it easier for them to do so. By contrast, the greater the effort required of citizens to become involved the less likely they are to do so.

Citizens' motivation to become involved as a co-producer will, in turn, depend on the importance or salience of the service provided. Is it a very important service for them, their family, loved-ones, a relative, a friend, or not? This will reflect how the service affects them, their life and life chances. Does it make a direct impact on their life and/or life chances, or does it only have an indirect effect? If and when a person feels that a service is very important for them and/or their loved-ones or vital to their life chances they will be more highly motivated to become involved in the co-production of it.

It is, therefore, necessary to make a distinction between enduring and non-enduring social services (Pestoff, 2012). Many social services belong to the former category and, therefore, have an immediate impact on the life, life chances and quality of life of the persons and/or families receiving them. The importance and impact of such services guarantee high client interest in their development especially in their quality. Enduring social services include: childcare or preschool services, basic and higher education, elder care, handicap care and housing as well as preventative, and long-term health care.

The Co-operative Gambit: Why Citizens Engage in Collective Action[11]

The pursuit of self-interest can either be individual or collective. In the latter there is an element of common benefit, not found in the former. Collective action and even more so collective interaction have the ability to transform the pursuit of self- interest into something more than the sum of individual self-interests. It makes possible the achievement of common goals that would otherwise be impossible for isolated, unorganized individuals. Such goals can include good quality primary education, good quality pre-school services, good quality health care, elder care, etc., at a reasonable cost to individuals and society.

---

[11] This phrase is taken from Victor Pestoff's paper "Co-production and Third Sector Social Services in Europe: Some Concepts and Evidence" (2012).

Collective action can help solve social and personal dilemmas, created either by the lack of some important social services on the market or by the variable quality of such services provided by the state. The lack of good quality childcare services in Ireland is a prime example. The local authorities don't provide them, or enough of them in many counties and the market simply prices them out of reach of most citizens. Thus, many families struggle to combine their professional career demands with family needs, particularly for high quality childcare. Many of them then reason that if they don't join hands with other like-minded persons to form an association and provide the service themselves, it simply won't be available to them.

If the market cannot provide an adequate amount of the service at affordable prices for most citizens, or if the quality of standardized public services is not acceptable to some citizens, they can come together to form an association to provide it both for themselves and for others.. Thus, without collective action a particular service would not be made readily available, or it would not be available at the level of quality desired by some groups. Therefore, in spite of well-known hurdles to collective action, without engaging in it no suitable childcare service will be provided for a number of concerned families.

Government understanding of this social and personal dilemma and acceptance of social economy alternatives may also prove crucial for success. A cooperative gambit is the willingness of individuals to sacrifice their short-term personal interest for the sake of the long-term individual and group benefits stemming from collective action in order to achieve a group goal or provide a social service. A social cooperative or social enterprise can create trust that helps to surmount the limits of the short-term personal interest of group members or to curb "free-riding". This encourages them to contribute their time, effort and other resources to achieve the fruits of their collective efforts that cannot be achieved by isolated individuals. Of course not everyone is willing to participate in collective action, but there may be enough of them to make it worth considering why some do

This chapter contends that while the introduction of a public policy framework facilitating the expansion of social economies in Ireland remains a distinct possibility there are a number of constraints that may mitigate the transformational outcomes Wright and Ostrom outline.

Suggestions for Policy Makers

The majority of evidence available to date, in particular that disseminated by the EU, OECD and UNRISD, suggests that there are a number of key areas that should be addressed to facilitate the social economy. These include:

- The legal, fiscal and regulatory frameworks;
- The development of sources of sustainable finance;
- Investment in human capital.

Specific enabling environments (legal, fiscal, regulatory) might be needed according to the form that their initiatives take. Social enterprises, like associations or co-operatives, need an ad-hoc legal status and regulatory measures designed to allow them to fulfil their social and economic goals, while pursuing medium and long-term sustainability on the market (OECD, 2010; UNRISD, 2014; Utting *et al.,* 2014).

The EU has suggested that a social capital marketplace should be fostered. Policy measures could include offering fiscal incentives to attract investors; offering multiple forms of credit enhancement; and, spearheading and monitoring innovative institutional arrangements between civil society, governments and financial institutions. Seed funding is critical in the early phases of a project as it covers the costs linked to a start- up and also the costs of capital investments. This could be provided through small loans or grants.

Investment in human capital has two distinct dimensions. The first relates to providing training opportunities to social entrepreneurs and including social entrepreneurship in school and university curricula. This arises because social entrepreneurs might need special training to help them hone and develop their entrepreneurial and creative skills.

The second dimension relates to the provision of training opportunities for public officials in the area of public tenders. Public procurement measures can be further developed so that social enterprises can consolidate and expand their growth. European procurement law allows local authorities to insert certain social clauses in their procurement procedures terms of reference, for example to encourage the employment of long-term unemployed or disadvantaged people. Involving social enterprises in public service delivery can bring many community benefits. However, public officials are often not well acquainted with those benefits, while some small social enterprises are not familiar with the public tendering process and need skills and networks to successfully compete in public bids. Training, both for public officials working on procurement and for social enterprises, should be provided and encouraged.

Conclusions

This chapter contends that public policy facilitating the expansion of the social economy in Ireland remains a distinct possibility. As Amin observes, "governments around the world, supported by parties and institutions of varying political hue, have begun to introduce legislation and policies to stimulate and support the social economy" (2009: 5). This change is not only linked to the ongoing economic crises but also stems from a "desire to make capitalism more caring through markets and modes of delivery that are socially responsible, needs-based and stakeholder-oriented" (2009: 5). In addition there is a very distinct discourse on the 'moral economy', that is "the norms which govern or should govern economic activity" (Sayer, 2000: 1). In Ireland this aspect of the debate has largely been mainstreamed by President Higgins' Ethics Initiative. It is feasible to enable the social economy in Ireland and Wales as a key component of a more sustainable and human-centred model of economic development. This process must be embedded in a public dialogue, detailing the role and nature of the social economy, how social economy stakeholders perceive themselves, how state and market actors and institutions perceive them and how an implementable policy framework might be developed. Ireland and Wales can avoid what Roberto Unger refers to as the "dictatorship of no alternatives" (2009: 1).

CHAPTER 3
EDUCATION TO ENABLE SOCIAL CHANGE!

Liann Buckley and Aifric O'Malley

Introduction to Social Enterprise at the DCU Ryan Academy
The DCU Ryan Academy for Entrepreneurs bridges the gap between academia and entrepreneurial practice. The Academy is a unique partnership between Ireland's leading young university, Dublin City University and the family of one of our greatest entrepreneurs, Tony Ryan. Education at the DCU Ryan Academy covers a range of programmes to educate and develop entrepreneurs in every sector including social enterprise.

Social enterprise is at the heart of the Academy, forming a key pillar of the overall strategy. The vision is to contribute to social change through the education of social entrepreneurs and managers of social enterprises, aiding in the development of sustainable social enterprises. At the DCU Ryan Academy, we want to help demonstrate that the social enterprise model is a viable, sustainable and achievable means of solving some of society's major social and environmental issues.

The Academic Approach to Social Enterprise
Education is essential in the development of sustainable social enterprises. Social enterprises operate within a commercial sphere; trading and using business models to deliver on their social mission. The social missions of these enterprises are as wide and varied as the business models they use to generate revenue.

We believe in the social enterprise model. Through education we can enable social entrepreneurs and social enterprise managers to gain the skills that will assist them on their journey to sustainability. Social entrepreneurs have endless passion for social change. Alone, this will not result in sustainable businesses but when coupled with the knowledge and skills to develop and implement best practice; social entrepreneurs learn to harness their ideas and develop businesses that will impact on communities and contribute significantly to the economy in which they operate.

We envisage the creation of a hub of social enterprise research hoping to stimulate the creation of new management theories and frameworks across the public, non-profit and for-profit sectors.

The Funding Opportunity

We matched our social enterprise values with NorDubCo and with Bangor University and Business in the Community Wales to form a partnership that allowed us to develop an initiative that changed the face of social enterprise education in Ireland and Wales.

This initiative was granted funding from the European Regional Development Fund through the Ireland Wales Programme 2007-2013 (INTERREG 4A) in February 2012. The Menter Iontach Nua initiative was designed to offer a creative and innovative approach to social enterprise education in Ireland and Wales reflecting sector needs and the values of the partners involved. The initiative incorporated mentoring and networking opportunities along with education to create significant benefit to the enterprises and individuals that engaged with it. The funding received through the Ireland Wales Programme enabled the design and development of a Masters' programme in social enterprise which was to be offered to eligible participants in the INTERREG regions of Ireland and Wales.

This was in the context of the recognition by all partners, that while there was no shortage of enthusiastic people wanting to start-up and support social enterprises, there was a disconnect between this and the requisite skills needed to bring an idea from embryonic stage to a viable business.

The Design of the Programme

The Menter Iontach Nua project enlisted the expertise of their Irish and Welsh steering groups and held meetings with them to determine the needs of the social enterprise sector. Bearing the outcomes of these meetings in mind and after conducting further research with the broader sector, the programme was designed to give participants an understanding of the theoretical and practical aspects of social enterprise while encouraging and enabling innovation.

The programme incorporated the best of business practices and managerial disciplines and aimed to maximise the potential of the participants involved and the social impact they could have. According to the Forfás report 'Social Enterprise in Ireland: Sectoral Opportunities and Policy Issues', published in 2013, on average 64 per cent of a social enterprise's total expenditure is spent on labour. This signifies that social enterprises are heavily involved in job creation and therefore a necessary skill is human resource management. HR along with subjects such as marketing, creativity and innovation, business strategy, social enterprise development and accounting ensure participants are primed to create effective and sustainable social impact.

Menter Iontach Nua also designed a series of community programmes and events to promote the sharing of knowledge with the wider social enterprise sector in Ireland and Wales. The vision for the project was to create an eco-system that would enable people to tackle some of the world's most intractable social and environmental issues.

The Story of the Participants

Applications for the Masters programme opened in August 2012. Within three weeks we had received over 380 expressions of interest in the programme, reinforcing the view that there was demand and need for training specific to the sector. The quality of the applications made for a tough review process with only 40 places available. However, the review committee chose to offer 44 people the opportunity to undertake the programme.

On the 23rd September 2012, 44 participants arrived at the DCU Ryan Academy in Dublin to start their two year journey on the MSc in Management (Innovation in Social Enterprise). The participants came from a range of organisations including social enterprises, community and voluntary organisations and public sector support agencies. This diversity was a fundamental element of the programme and the foundation for the future creation of a network of leaders to ensure the development of the sector in both Ireland and Wales.

The Teaching

On the 1st October 2012 the Menter Iontach Nua team, along with the Dublin City University Business School, delivered the very first online lecture to the now virtual students in their homes and offices across Ireland and Wales.

The initial concept was to stream the lecture in real time as it happened in the Business School. However this did not work out and the first set of lectures were recorded and watched later by the students. But this was not the student experience that had been envisaged and both the needs and solutions had to be revisited. The overarching consensus was that there was a need to recreate the classroom experience and enable the participants to have the same experience as those that were attending lectures on campus. The solution was to change the technology and use new tools and techniques to build their network to ensure that they felt connected to the university and their peers while studying.

Outside of the virtual classroom, participants from Ireland and Wales collaborated on projects and gained not only vital skills in technology but also the benefits of sharing knowledge and experience across borders. Using the online forums, participants gave group presentations, created apps, managed Google AdWords campaigns and discussed the challenges, benefits and opportunities for social enterprise at length.

The Impact

This programme has had an impact on a number of levels, firstly on the field of social enterprise research, secondly on the individual participant and their organisation and finally on the development of the sector in both Ireland and Wales.

In relation to the field of social enterprise research, the future potential and impact of the programme was clearly evident on the 29th of August 2014 when participants showcased their course work to an audience in DCU. The showcase reflected the wealth of research, (some of which is highlighted in this book), which has been generated by the programme in the area of social enterprise. Research topics included; brand personality, volunteer management, housing, financial sustainability, homecare services, care farming, disability employment and social enterprise networks.

When considering the impact the programme had on the individual participant it is illustrated best by a direct quote from an individual participant. Guy Evans was a participant from Wales who, reflecting on his experience on the programme said:

When I came into the charity, I was very much wearing a woolly jumper, wanting to hug trees and save the world, that end of the market. Now I'm leaning, a little uncomfortably, toward pinstripe, but the reality of the situation is that through using the business skills and confidence I've gained, I know that the enterprises we've developed are reaching more people. We are now working with considerably more people than we did before I went on the Masters.

The programme as described above was designed for this purpose, to enable social enterprises to increase their social impact and sustainability through innovation and the application of business practices.

One of the primary aims of the programme was to build social capital within the sector. Strong social capital produces significant benefits by enabling the flow of knowledge and resources and allowing organisations to better react to challenges and identify opportunities. We believe it has achieved this through both the network of participants and the involvement of the wider sector in the project activities. Samantha Richardson a participant from Waterford identified that:

> *This course has developed a network of leaders, who have skills in different areas of the social enterprise sector, and this is the first time now that there is a unified voice in Ireland and Wales who can progress and advance the sector in a way that has never happened before.*

The Learning
On completion of the programme the following learning has been identified from the experience of the Menter Iontach Nua project team:

- Education is a key tool in enabling social change. By educating people with the skills and knowledge to create sustainable social enterprises they can impact significantly on the people, environment and economy of the communities in which they live and work;
- The key to successful online learning is the recreation of the benefits of classroom learning. Using virtual classrooms and online tools enables the participant to stay connected and build networks with their teachers and peers;
- All programme elements and schedules should ideally be structured to suit the online learner's needs. In the instance of this Masters programme the average student was working full time and had family commitments. Therefore, the ideal schedule for

lectures would be evenings with the recorded option available to view at a later date;

- Business skills are transferable. However modules should incorporate, where possible, sector specific case studies and examples. Context is also a key element for successful delivery of business modules to the social enterprise learner;
- It is important to encourage and facilitate the interaction between students online. If this factor is not taken into consideration in an online learning environment, the opportunity, for not only building a network but, for effectively sharing knowledge may be lost;
- By improving the professionalism of those working in social enterprises the financial sustainability of the organisation and the impact of the sector as a whole can be increased.

Recommendations

Following on the experience and the learning achieved on completion of the first two year Master's Programme, we have produced a series of recommendations as follows:

- All courses are underpinned by a commitment to innovation and social change;
- Programmes offered to online students are flexible and structured around their needs;
- Where possible all modules are made sector specific using case studies and real life examples;
- All opportunities for participant interaction and engagement should be taken advantage of;
- Research be shared with the wider sector, both nationally and globally, to encourage development;
- Efforts to build a dynamic network of national and international social entrepreneurs should be continued.

Now we are doing it all over again

From the success of the Menter Iontach Nua programme, DCU will continue to offer level 9 education in Innovation in Social Enterprise. There will be an emphasis on best business practices and managerial skills, helping to solve pressing social challenges. The graduates will gain the knowledge and skills needed to participate effectively at leadership level in the decision-making and management of social enterprises and will develop a capacity to respond creatively to the needs and problems of the wider community.

CHAPTER 4
HARNESSING THE POWER OF A COLLECTIVE SOCIAL ENTERPRISE MOVEMENT IN IRELAND

Bebhinn Hare, Giustina Francesca Mizzoni, Roy O'Connor, Breffni O'Rourke and Eoghan Stack

Introduction

This chapter details the main findings and recommendations of a practicum undertaken with the Irish Social Enterprise Network (ISEN). ISEN is establishing a network for social enterprises and would-be social enterprises in Ireland. Our research set out to ascertain the key features and activities required to successfully build a network of social enterprises in an uncertain environment.

The dynamics of the current environment in which ISEN operates is one which has not yet reached a 'steady state' as the Irish social enterprise sector is relatively new and still emerging. The sector itself lacks clear definition and identity, it is not well-funded and the broader non-profit sector has been damaged by scandal and austerity measures and also suffers from a lack of private funding infrastructure (O'Neill, 2014; The Wheel, 2009; Aikins, 2009). These factors all combine to create a sector which is fluid and full of uncertainty.

This chapter provides a brief overview of ISEN and the opportunity which exists for its development, due in part to the lack of an agreed definition of social enterprise in Ireland. It provides a review of the literature around network formation, specifically that on inter-organisational networks and their performance benefits for all types of enterprise and on the importance of governance and marketing in creating a strong and vibrant social enterprise network.

ISEN and Opportunity

The Irish Social Enterprise Network (ISEN) was set up in 2013 and aspires to be "an indispensable resource to everyone in Ireland that is interested in social enterprise" (ISEN, 2013). ISEN's mission is to make the Irish social enterprise sector much more visible, through directing people and social enterprises to the relevant resources, supports and information that they need.

Brouard and Larivet (2011) assert that there appears to be no universally agreed definition of social enterprise and, indeed, many different definitions are to be found in academic literature. According to Doyle and Lalor the question of definition is important for the development of social enterprises as the "ideological perspective of individuals and organisations relating to social enterprise will influence the boundaries of activities in which social entrepreneurs engage" (2012: 5). Pearse too argues that a clear and unambiguous definition of social enterprises is absolutely essential but further argues that first it is necessary to build the vision and values of what social enterprises will mean to society, "Too often social enterprises are coy about their values and play them down, pretending that they are really the same as other businesses but just happen to have a social purpose" (2003: 146). He claims the development of a movement, with networking opportunities and relationships of trust, is essential to create a shared vision based on those values.

ISEN is at a juncture in its lifecycle where uncertainty in the sector could be turned to opportunity. A void exists in Ireland for a strong credible voice to take a leadership role around social enterprise; ISEN has the capacity to fulfil this role, and in doing so, to support a small sector with the potential to fully blossom.

Networks
The prevailing view is that inter-organizational networking (group to group / organisation to organisation) is essential to business success (Zaheer *et al.*, 2010; Akkermans, 2001). Firms are not autonomous and self-reliant entities, they rely on linkages with other firms to access capabilities and resources. This view perceives organisational action as essentially relational. Within inter-organisational networks there are a number of different theoretical perspectives as to how and why they develop: resources, trust, power and/or status (Bergenholtz and Waldstrom, 2011), as presented in Table 1 below. Also, the relationships within these networks can be extremely diverse such as joint ventures, alliances, strategic networks and interlocks or franchising (Bergenholtz and Waldstrom, 2011).

Table 1: Theoretical perspectives on inter-organisational networks

Resources	Most often for access to information and for richer information the structure should be rich, as in Burt's 'structural holes' theory. Networks are extremely useful for organisations seeking reliable exchange of intangibles such as knowledge and know how (Qureshi, 1995).
Trust	Most agree trust is an essential aspect (Zaheer *et al.*, 2010; Akkermans, 2001), particularly in the sharing of information resources (Mentzas *et al.*, 2006). The stronger the connection the higher the level of trust with an associated drop in transactional costs.
Power	Networks can constrain and/or increase power (Zaheer *et al.*, 2010)
Status	Membership of a network is a signalling mechanism, inferring the quality of a firm through the quality of its relationships (Zaheer *et al.*, 2010)

Carlsson (2003) asserts that information and knowledge are vital resources. According to Mu *et al.*, (2008) knowledge creation and sharing are processes that cannot be induced through coercion; rather they are social processes facilitated by social capital. Since knowledge can be a source of competitive advantage, creating communities that share knowledge is a social challenge (Widén-Wulff and Ginman, 2004).

In their empirical study Chiu *et al.* (2006) found that shared vision was positively related to the quality of knowledge shared on the network. Further it is argued that a shared vision amongst network members, leads to sharing of resources (Tsai and Ghoshai, 1998). Shared goals, interests and vision facilitate a community to understand more fully the meaning of knowledge sharing (Chiu *et al.*, 2006). Hence common goals and norms is a binding force that creates trust (Tsai and Ghoshai, 1998) which is an enabler for social exchange and cooperation and opens people up to knowledge sharing. It facilitates cooperation which in turn begets trust (Nahapiet and Ghoshai, 1998). This all points to the importance and necessity of stating clearly and unambiguously what the objectives are in bringing together partners and the purpose in seeking the exchange of knowledge.

Demonstrating Shared Values and Generating Trust through Governance

As indicated in the European EMES definition (Table 2 below), it is often assumed that social enterprise in Europe, as opposed to in the United States, involves some work or participatory contribution by those benefiting from the programming, for example worker cooperatives. The European emphasis on participation also extends to the management of the social enterprise. According to Young and Salamon "In Europe, the notion of social enterprise focuses more heavily on the way an organisation is governed and what its purpose is rather than on whether it strictly adheres to the non-distribution constraint of a formal non-profit organisation" (2002: 433); (see also Borzaga and Santuari, 1998). The significance of the governance of a social enterprise in the European context is identified in six key principles of a social enterprise identified by Pearse (2005), two of which are focused on governance, they being that: assets are held in trust for the benefit of the community; and the social enterprises are accountable to their constituency, usually adopting a form of democratic governance.

Pearse describes governance as being "a democratic structure where its constituents can join as members and elect a majority of its board/management committee" (2005: 3). Within the literature on governance there are two main theories: one based on stewardship which is concerned with maximising financial performance; and the other based on stakeholder which is concerned with enabling democratic participation from involved organisations (Low, 2006). Participants in a discussion group, undertaken as part of the primary research for this chapter, specifically highlighted the importance of governance: they called for the voice of members to be heard but facilitated within a democratic structure.

Any new sectoral network intending to be a model for social enterprises should give consideration to adopting a stakeholder model of governance. This should be a robust model using a combination of individual and collective ownership with the purpose of embedding long term interests. This approach binds the fortunes of all stakeholders to the sustainability of the enterprise (Major and Boby, 2000).

Adopting a stakeholder model at an early stage establishes a standard, enabling the demonstration of commitment to transparent corporate governance and creating a space where strong collaboration can be facilitated, thus giving legitimacy to the body as a lobbying and advocacy network. Becoming an organisation which is predicated on its members interests will, not only enable the legitimate representation of Irish social enterprise, but will also ensure accountability to the members and the sector.

Table 2: Some definitions of Social Enterprise

Social Enterprise Alliance (USA)	Social enterprises are businesses whose primary purpose is the common good. They use the methods and disciplines of business and the power of the marketplace to advance their social, environmental and human justice agendas. (Social Enterprise Alliance, 2014)
Voluntary code of practice for social enterprise in Scotland	A social enterprise (SE) is a business trading in the marketplace – selling goods and services – but whose primary objective is to achieve social and/or environmental benefit. Regardless of its legal form, the constitution of an SE will include the requirement that profits are reinvested in the business or in the beneficiary community - and not distributed to owners/shareholders/ investors. The constitution will always require that, on dissolution the assets of the SE are reinvested in another organisation with similar aims and objectives. SEs are differentiated from charities and voluntary organisations which do not aspire to financial independence through trading. They are also distinct from the public sector and cannot be the subsidiary of a public body (Voluntary Code of Practice for Social Enterprise in Scotland, 2014)
EMES (Europe)	A social enterprise has: • A continuous activity producing goods and/or selling services; • A high degree of autonomy; • A significant level of economic risk; • A minimum amount of paid work; • An explicit aim to benefit the community; • An initiative launched by a group of citizens; • A decision-making power not based on capital ownership; • A participatory nature, which involves the persons affected by the activity; • Limited profit distribution (EMES, 2014).
Forfás (Ireland)	A social enterprise is "… an enterprise that trades for a social / societal purpose, where at least part of its income is earned from its trading activity, is separate from Government, and where the surplus is primarily re-invested in the social objective." (Forfás, 2013)

The Research Approach

The aim of our research was to ascertain which organisations would be most supportive of a network, specifically of a network organisation such as ISEN, and would therefore value a network more highly. The research conducted was both qualitative and quantitative in nature, consisting of three distinct pieces of primary research – a survey of the attendees at ISEN's inaugural conference, a World Café style group at the same event and a second survey of the attendees at an ISEN Speaker Series event.

ISEN Conference Survey

The attendees at the inaugural Irish Social Enterprise Conference in February 2014 were surveyed with a view to gaining an insight into potential customer segmentation opportunities. The intention was to gauge identification with 'social enterprise' to determine if this had any effect on perceptions of ISEN and its services, in this instance through the intention to pay for future events.

Key Findings

47 per cent of respondents to the survey identified with social enterprise with 78 per cent of that group engaged in trading activities. The most notable results were that current trading activity and identification with the label of social enterprise[12] are the main influencing factors on the types of potential network member organisations willing to pay to attend futures ISEN event. The segment most likely to pay for events are *established organisations* (2+ years) that identify with social enterprise and are trading. We found that the least likely to pay to participate in ISEN events are *pre-start-up organisations*, those that identify with social enterprise but are not yet trading. None of this cohort indicated a willingness to pay to attend an ISEN event.

ISEN Conference World Café

The conference hosted a World Café event in the second half of the day with five key questions set for discussion, one of which was developed by our research team. The basic format of a World Café event requires participants to rotate every 15 minutes from table to table, each getting

---

[12] In these findings the phrase 'identify with social enterprise' denotes those respondents that self-identify as social enterprises as well as those that have a dual identify, i.e. charity with social enterprise activity.

an opportunity to voice their thoughts and opinions on the five topics. The dynamic nature of the event meant that a verbatim recording of individual responses was not possible but an analysis was conducted on the written reports completed by the facilitators and scribes.

The question we posed to the approximately 80 participants at the World Café was:

> *Over the course of the day you have heard from both an existing social enterprise network (Scottish Network) and what ISEN has to offer. What would you/your organisation expect from a social enterprise network?*

Key findings
Responses were classified according to resource type, influenced by the identification of resource access as a key benefit of inter-organisational networks, and the contents of each resource category was refined to a small number of overall 'benefit' or 'value' statements which are required by potential members of the network (Table 3). The World Café group participants also identified that the uncertainty of the sector is of concern to those operating within it and called for articulation of values to be made.

Table 3: Benefits statements of each resource category

Resource type:	Benefit required by potential customers
Physical	*Events across the country and office space for starting up.*
Organisational	*Coordinated networking with regular and relevant communications.*
Human Assets and Intellectual Capital	*Knowledge sharing and idea incubation. Knowing how to start-up and run a social enterprise.*
Brand, image and reputational assets	*Representation to government; social enterprise friendly policies; increased exposure of social enterprise.*
Relationships	*Cost-savings through sharing, bartering and inter-trading; access to new markets and connections beyond the sector.*
Organisational culture and incentive system	*Cohesion, articulation of shared values and a vision for the sector.*

Findings here indicated that those already active within the social enterprise sector value ISEN more highly. . They provided key segmentation data and information on the key benefits required by those operating within, or aspiring to operate within, the social enterprise sector in Ireland.

Marketing Strategy Development

The lack of an agreed definition of social enterprise makes measurement of the market a challenge. We came to the conclusion that correct classification of organisation type etc. as 'social enterprise or 'non-social enterprise' would be somewhat of a red herring in the development of a Marketing Strategy.

From our primary research, five key customer segments were identified. The segments were named by the research team for easy identification during the design of the strategy. The details of the segments, key features and names are listed in Table 4.

Table 4: Identified customer segments

Segment identified	Key Features	Name
Established trading organisations which identify with social enterprise (these include charities with social enterprise activity and both established (2+ years) and start-up (0-2 years).	Self-identification with social enterprise and any level of trading activity.	*Up and Running*
Trading organisations of any type with an interest in the Social enterprise model or social sectors.	Do not identify with social enterprise, do trade, have a vested interest in becoming involved in the network.	*Spend Money to Make Money*
Charities with the intention to move into social enterprise activities: made up of charities currently funded primarily through fundraising and/or through private/government grants.	Do not identify with social enterprise but are examining options to trade for the first time due to funding constraints. Two thirds are willing to pay for events.	*Just Trying It Out*
Pre-start-up social enterprises, those with intention to trade, predominantly social entrepreneurs with no current funding.	Self-identify with social enterprise, no traded income, unwillingness to pay, require physical and knowledge resources.	*Show Me The Money*
Academic institutions and students	No great willingness to pay but very interested in becoming involved in the social enterprise can provide knowledge resources.	*Knowledge is Power*

37

Targeting

Attractiveness of the segments was analysed (Figure 1) in terms of short-term income potential and the expenditure of resources 'effort' involved in accessing this income (payment for events and/or membership fees).

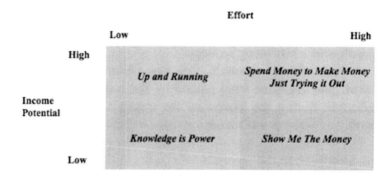

Figure 1 Analysis of attractiveness of ISEN customer segments

Due to the high level of interest *'Up and Running'* hold in paying for ISEN events combined with the fact that they are already established trading organisations, this segment is judged to be the most attractive for ISEN to target as members.[13]

While *'Spend Money to Make Money'* and *'Just Trying It Out'* segments have high potential to be ISEN member segments, a high degree of effort would be involved to convert these to active membership due to the level of persuasion required. We concluded that ISEN should develop a longer-term strategy to attract these segments in the future.

'Knowledge is Power' is an attractive segment as a resource to ISEN both as creator of knowledge and as a support to ISEN in increasing the number and level of its activities and events. Association with academic institutions would also assist in raising ISEN's credibility within the sector. This segment is therefore of both short and long-term benefit.

'Show Me the Money' has been identified as a poor choice of segment in the short-term due to the identified lack of willingness to pay for

---

[13] Although the surveys split this group into 0-2 years and 2+ year segments our research showed no significant difference between the two groups and they have been selected as one segment. Further segmentation of this group is recommended as further opportunities for market research become available.

events or to pay higher membership rates. However, as members of this segment have the potential to grow into trading social enterprises; it is a segment which should be nurtured but with minimal resource commitments.

And so *Up and Running* and *Knowledge is Power* were identified as the key short-term target segments as they have enough buy-in to the sector and ideals of social enterprise that they can become part of ISEN's resources through network relations.

Positioning

We recommend positioning to attract the *Up and Running* segment through the development of a clearer statement of principles surrounding social enterprise, with a concurrent communications campaign about the move toward a membership based organisation. This positioning would draw on the network perspectives discussed above through the articulation of shared values. As already indicated from the literature, clearly articulated values serve to attract those that share them, resulting in greater trust between network actors and increasing the sharing and quality of knowledge resources.

The communication of internal governance changes is also important in terms of positioning. In order to legitimately claim to share values, networks must be seen to demonstrate those values themselves. An inability or unwillingness to communicate these changes risks damaging the impact of the marketing position.

Relationship Marketing Strategy

Influenced by the literature on network formation, we developed a relationship marketing strategy with a view to harnessing network relationships so that the members create benefits for each other, rather that the network organisation aiming to provide all of the benefits through their own activities. The main thrust of the relationship marketing strategy is to employ a true 'network approach' and use partnerships and collaborations to assist ISEN to provide required member benefits. Developing partnerships is inextricably linked with marketing activity, specifically 'relationship marketing' where every customer is an individual, strong customer relationships are important and knowledge of the individual customer is paramount (Donaldson and O'Toole, 2002).

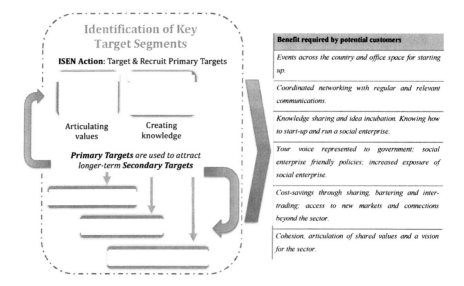

Figure 2 Relationship Marketing Strategy

This approach requires the development of a small number of relationships with key identified targets from the *Up and Running* and *Knowledge is Power* segments. For instance *Knowledge is Power* can generate online knowledge resources which direct *Show Me the Money* to the more tangible benefit of 'office space for starting up'. Volunteer Champions are recruited from the *Up and Running* segment that can articulate ISEN values at events across the country, helping to create the benefit of 'cohesion, articulation of values and a shared vision of the sector'. In creating the segments, the actions of both segments have the added value of increasing the sense of trust in potential members and in increasing the strength of the social enterprise sector through social capital.

Recommendations

Our recommendations to tackle uncertainty within the market are as follows:

- Provide clarity around an informed definition of social enterprise;
- Encourage existing social enterprises to recognise themselves under this banner;
- Form a network of social enterprises that supports individual members and advances the cause through collective strength;

- Alter the governance structure to increase accountability.

A strong and clear vision is important to increase the strength of a network. While this may be challenging for new social enterprise networks given the debate and uncertainty attached to social enterprise, as has been shown, an articulation of shared vision and values can increase the trust between network actors that identify with these values. Trust and resource access can also be increased by ISEN through careful choice of governance and network form (open/closed).

There is justification for ISEN positioning itself as the voice of social enterprise through providing a clear statement concerning what it considers to be the defining 'principles' of social enterprise or developing a definition itself. While these principles should be confidently communicated they can still be flexible in order to accommodate shifts in values among networks members.

As well as providing opportunities to leverage scarce resources from one another, partnerships and collaboration within the social enterprise sector can also contribute to the development of ISEN itself. Our recommendations require an acceptance of an open structure based on a stakeholder model and on open collaboration with a membership that itself articulates values, a true 'network' approach. Through the members' own articulation of values more network members are drawn to join, thus increasing the opportunities for social capital within the network.

CHAPTER 5
INNOVATE BALLYMUN: SUSTAINING SOCIAL ENTERPRISE IN AREAS OF DISADVANTAGE

Séamus Carlin, Paul Murgatroyd, Nóirín Coghlan, Alan Breathnach

Introduction

This research study focuses on the financial sustainability of social enterprises in an area of social disadvantage. It investigates specifically what supports and resources are needed by social enterprises in the Ballymun area of North Dublin, in order to ensure their financial sustainability. Whilst the study was set within the childcare sector, the issues which are identified are of relevance to any social enterprise operating in Ireland or further afield, primarily in relation to the level of resources and supports required by social enterprises to sustain their work. In this context the research proposes a financial sustainability toolkit that can be implemented pragmatically across social enterprises and which includes Finance; Management; Quality; and Strategy solutions.

Through the lens of the childcare sector the research examines the State's role in supporting social enterprise and shows a funding system no longer fit for purpose. It also addresses the quality versus cost aspect of sustaining childcare services in the current funding model in Ireland. In addition, it considers the issues around measures of prevention versus intervention investments in childcare; the turbulent policy and funding environment; sustainable mixed income streams and business models; profitability versus sustainability; and adoption of best practice in sustaining social enterprises. Finally, the research illustrates some of the gaps in the literature on the financial sustainability of social enterprise and highlights the 'definition debate' with regard to the meaning of 'social enterprise, concluding that it remains a contested space and the subject of on-going discourse in Ireland and beyond.

Research Context and Background

This research was undertaken as part of a practicum project in the MSc in Management (Innovation in Social Enterprise) at Dublin City

University. It was sponsored by Innovate Ballymun[14], an independent 'think tank' encouraging creative collaboration through individual and organisational involvement which serves to promote new sustainable partnerships for the social and economic benefit of the local community and others. Innovate Ballymun is led by the Ballymun Whitehall Area Partnership in conjunction with Dublin City University and Dublin City Council. The research objective was to investigate what supports and resources are needed by social enterprises in the Ballymun area of Dublin, in order to ensure their financial sustainability. The concept of social enterprise used was as per the Forfás[15] (2013) definition and classification of social enterprise in Ireland. Ultimately, the research explores the concept of financial sustainability for social enterprises, focusing specifically on the childcare sector within the Ballymun area.

In the first instance a review of the literature on social enterprise, childcare policy, economic development and financial sustainability was undertaken and served to set the research context. Whilst much has been written in the areas reviewed, there is a dearth of empirical evidence and academic insight on financial sustainability within social enterprise specifically. Thus, the intention was to add to knowledge and insight in this area and to highlight the emerging themes and issues in an Irish context which may resonate with practitioners and academics in other jurisdictions further afield.

Presentation of Empirical Research
The research methodology involved a five-stage process and the use of a combination of quantitative and qualitative methods. Through this process, the authors built-up a picture of the financial sustainability issues facing social enterprises in the Ballymun area. The research was located within an interpretative paradigm, with multiple perspectives engaged and subsequently reflected so as to illuminate different elements of the study and subsequently triangulate our research findings. Thus, we aligned ourselves with Myers view of interpretive researchers as assuming "that access to reality (given or socially

---

[14] Innovate Ballymun www.innovateballymun.org
[15] A social enterprise is an enterprise: that trades for a social/societal purpose; where at least part of its income is earned from its trading activity; is separate from government; and where the surplus is primarily re-invested in the social objective.

constructed) is only through social constructions such as language, consciousness, shared meanings, and instruments" (Myers, 2008: 38).

The five stage process involved the use of the following instruments: an online survey of childcare providers; a series of semi-structured interviews and further structured interviews with key stakeholders i.e. funders, policymakers, practitioners and support agencies in childcare operating across Ireland; two case studies which were used to inform best practice regarding the financial sustainability of social enterprise and, finally, analysis of the financial accounts of childcare providers and calculation of relevant ratios to understand their financial stability.

Key Findings

From the perspective of stakeholders in the childcare sector, the qualitative research identified four main issues:

- A lack of agreed understanding as to what constitutes a social enterprise;
- The importance of high quality childcare provision;
- The challenges of financial sustainability;
- The need for additional supports - both financial and non-financial.

From the perspective of childcare providers in the sector, the issues identified were:

- The extent or otherwise to which childcare providers see themselves as social enterprises;
- The importance of strong governance and operational management;
- The key role that additional supports such as labour market activation schemes play in contributing to financial sustainability;
- The impact on quality of service of the complex mix of children's needs in areas of disadvantage.

Sustainability Toolkit

The research identified four areas of concern which can be linked to Leon's (2001) four pillars of sustainability[16] and it devised what it has termed a 'Financial Sustainability Toolkit' (Figure 1) to address them. The measures proposed in the toolkit specifically address the issues

---

[16] The four pillars of sustainability include: 1) Strategic and financial planning; 2) Income diversification; 3) Sound administration and finance; 4) Own income generation.

(outlined above) identified by both the stakeholders and childcare providers within the sector. It is intended that the toolkit be of practical use to Innovate Ballymun childcare providers and, indeed, to other social enterprises in sustaining their work.

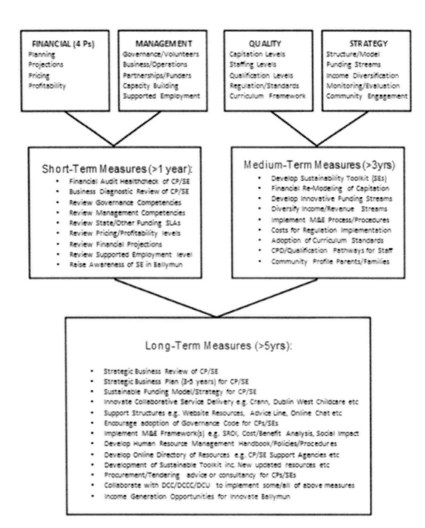

Figure 3: Financial Sustainability Toolkit for Childcare Social Enterprises[17],[18]

[17] Abbreviations: Childcare Provider (CP); Social Enterprise (SE); Monitoring and Evaluation (M&E); Service Level Agreement (SLA); Social Return on Investment (SROI); Dublin City Council (DCC); Dublin City Childcare Committee (DCCC); Dublin City University (DCU).

The areas of concern identified and addressed by the toolkit are those of Finance; Management; Quality and Strategy. These areas were identified by both the research findings and the literature reviewed around best practices and models of financial sustainability. As can be seen in Figure 1 each area of concern contains a number of components, all of which contribute towards achieving longer-term viability and sustainability of social enterprises. The selection of these components reflects the views of policymakers and practitioners in the sector.

As the toolkit illustrates, it is recommended that Innovate Ballymun focus on the set of measures on a short, medium and long term basis. In the short term (within one year) a review process should be conducted in line with the identified measures listed above. In the medium term (within three years) Innovate Ballymun should look to develop realistic support plans from a mix of the above measures. Longer term (within five years) a more focussed strategic approach, aligned to achieving financial sustainability of social enterprises, should be implemented in collaboration with other key stakeholders operating in the sector.

Prevention vs. Intervention

Our research has pointed to inadequate capitation funding levels, especially in the context of the complex needs of vulnerable families and children attending services in Ballymun. The literature points to a large body of evidence that supports the view that significant early investment in high quality childcare and early years education is required, particularly in services that cater for a high proportion of disadvantaged children. Quality matters because it promotes child development; provides family support and helps families to exit poverty through employment and training opportunities (Start Strong, 2014). Thus, it provides a greater Social Return on Investment (SROI).

Our research further shows that, given the current costs of intervention, coupled with the sustainability challenges of the childcare sector the surpluses/profits that providers are able to generate cannot meet the real costs associated with the regulatory environment and policy framework demands placed upon childcare providers to attain high quality and sustainable childcare into the future. Quality of early

---

[18] Adapted from A Conceptual Model of Financial Sustainability Challenges and Promising Practices for Non-profits Serving Low-Income Populations (Sontag-Padilla, et al., 2011).

childhood care and education matters for all children with the benefits being greatest for children from a disadvantaged background (Melhuish, 2004; OECD, 2012; Start Strong, 2013). Countries that achieve the double dividend of affordable and quality service delivery do so through public investment.

Funding vs. Business Models

Childcare providers continue to have difficulties in managing their day to day cash flow and struggle to control the capital and non-capital costs associated with running a high quality childcare organisation. In the context of promoting socio-economic development, existing budgetary cuts and a limited funding mix mean the current funding model is no longer fit-for-purpose. The government's funding policy and lack of shared inter-departmental responsibility does not sustain high quality childcare provision in the medium to longer-term.

In order to provide opportunities which will alleviate some of the pressure on the current fragile and unstable childcare business model, Innovate Ballymun may have to take a two tiered approach - seeking to empower the potential of social enterprise while acting as an advocate for the sector through dialogue with Government. In the case of Innovate Ballymun, the generation of a profit or surplus from providing childcare services to the community is not possible because of the combination of funding constraints, the complex mix of child and family needs; and the uncertain policy environment within which the sector operates.

Taking cognisance of this and other challenges facing the childcare sector in Ballymun, it would be prudent for Innovate Ballymun to explore the feasibility of other best practices and new business models of childcare, nationally and internationally. This with a view to developing a better understanding of local experiences, mapping the services and looking at the synergies and gaps across the non-profit sector in respect of financial sustainability so as to ensure that it plays a part is in Ballymun's future social and economic development.

One such model is that of Dublin West Childcare Services, an amalgamation of four childcare providers based in South County Dublin which is a replica of the Crann[19] model in County Meath. Both of these services were borne out of the need for community childcare

---

[19] Crann Support Group http://www.crannsupportgroup.ie

groups to be sustainable during difficult economic times. The service providers realised that, by working in partnership, they could achieve their common aim - the delivery of quality affordable childcare while remaining sustainable and retaining their own individual autonomy.

Trading and Sustaining Income

Largely due to continued uncertainty over Government funding, social enterprises in Ireland are focusing more and more on generating traded income sources or developing management capacity to adapt to a more enterprise-orientation, whilst retaining their social aims. The childcare sector is behind the curve in respect of developing a broader funding mix and tradable income streams. Whether childcare organisations adopt a social enterprise philosophy or develop a robust business model over time is of little consequence. However, what is of consequence is their limited understanding of the concept, requirements and more importantly, the opportunities that a social enterprise model can offer. Innovate Ballymun has the potential to contribute to the development of knowledge and understanding in that regard.

Profitability vs. Sustainability

To understand the differences in factors relating to financial sustainability between a for-profit and a non-profit organisation, it is important to identify and understand the long-term goals of the organisation. For instance, the ultimate strategic goal of for-profit organisations is to acquire profit and market share, whereas for non-profits' financial outcomes are merely a means to accomplishing an organisation's social mission (Hackler and Saxton, 2007).

Thus, a non-profit organisation's ability to pursue its mission (i.e. providing consistent and quality services) and its financial sustainability are inextricability linked. Financial sustainability refers to the ability to maintain financial capacity over time. Regardless of an organisation's for-profit or non-profit status, the challenges of establishing financial capacity and financial sustainability are central to organisational function (Bowman, 2011). Distinct from a traditional for-profit business model that focuses primarily on making a profit for the benefit of owners and shareholders, non-profits should make assessments in terms of their profitability and their social mission impact (Bell et al., 2010). Specifically, non-profits should determine whether or not their programme activities are producing the desired result (i.e. effectiveness) and whether the results are adequate in proportion to the cost of effort (i.e. efficiency). For non-profits, profitability reflects maintenance of working capital to support or continue operations of programs and services.

Defining Social Enterprise

Agreement exists amongst policymakers and academics that social enterprises play an increasing role in restructuring local economies and contributing to economic growth, social development and sustainability, which are core to Europe's economic strategy (Forfás, 2013; SEETF, 2012). Nevertheless, social enterprise is a contested term with little agreement about its definition and nature (Doyle, 2009; Pearce, 2003). The absence of an agreed definition amongst all the different key stakeholders can hinder the potential of social enterprises to be recognised by a range of stakeholders including state agencies, community, voluntary organisations and the private sector.

Agreement around definition is important from a range of perspectives. Firstly, from a policymakers' perspective it is vital to have clarity on what their funding is intended to develop and achieve (Forfás, 2013; Pearce, 2003; SEETF, 2012). Secondly, from an administrative point of view it is important to identify who will provide the funding (Forfás, 2013; SEETF, 2012). Thirdly, from an academic perspective is it important to clarify whether it is a sector or a system that is being researched (Pearce, 2003).

A UK study on services for children, young people and families explored the service providers' familiarity or otherwise with the concept of social enterprise and found that they did not identify themselves as such (Strang France, 2007). The interviews revealed various preconceptions and misconceptions about social enterprise (Strang France, 2007). This reflects our findings with various childcare providers and stakeholders alike. The UK study concluded that all of the organisations displayed innovative entrepreneurial activity but will require (outside) assistance in order to (build their capacity to) develop as social enterprises in order to deliver added value to children and young people (Strang France, 2007).

Conclusion

Childcare providers, as social enterprise organisations, have a key role to play in contributing to local economic development through the provision of quality affordable childcare services. Achieving and maintaining financial sustainability remains a challenge for the sector, given the evolving funding and policy landscape in Ireland, set against a backdrop of limited resources and increasing demand for services.

> *It's not enough [for social enterprises] to have a high-impact programme if there's no effective strategy for sustaining the organisation financially. And neither is it enough to be financially stable . . . yet surprisingly, in the non-profit sector, financial information and information about mission impact are seldom discussed in an integrated way* (Bell *et al.*, 2010: 3).

The challenges of maintaining financial sustainability while delivering a quality programme are exacerbated by other factors for organisations serving communities in need, as is the case in Ballymun. Childcare providers serving high-need or low-income, and sometimes minority populations or communities are faced with balancing multiple community challenges that reach far beyond the mission of the organisation. It is necessary for funding agencies and stakeholders to understand the interaction between the economic and the cultural in low-income communities and the challenges that social enterprises face in order to maximise strategies to ensure sustainability and ultimately improve services for the community.

Whilst our research findings are in line with other research in this field, we suggest that they also act as a foundation for further research and discussion on the contribution of financial sustainability of social enterprise, specifically within the context of socially disadvantaged areas.

At a strategic level, this research recommends a focus on evidence-based practice to support policymakers and social enterprises to make better informed decisions in order to achieve higher quality outcomes and impacts for all children, especially those in disadvantaged areas.

At an operational level, it is recommended that social enterprises adopt a financial sustainability approach and use the toolkit proposed and the resources at their disposal to meet their mission and sustain their work in the longer-term.

At a local level there is scope for policymakers, administrators and beneficiaries to come together and create a shared understanding of the role of childcare social enterprises in the social regeneration of Ballymun. It is recommended that a roundtable discussion take place to enhance dialogue between administrators, policymakers, funders and beneficiaries and to establish collective agreement on the types of supports necessary for childcare providers (as social enterprises) to reach their full potential. Innovate Ballymun is well placed to contribute and add value to the existing local initiatives and national structures.

CHAPTER 6
ARMIES, PRISONS AND CARE GARDENS: A FEASIBILITY STUDY INTO THE COMMERCIAL VIABILITY OF A SOCIAL ENTERPRISE LINKING IN TO WREXHAM PRISON

Sandra Ackers, Victoria Burrows, Anthony Hearn, Guy Hamilton Evans

Introduction

On the 27th June 2013 it was announced that the UK's largest prison was to be built in Wrexham, North Wales, and is scheduled to open in 2017. The £250 million development will house 2,100 male prisoners in what is described as a Category C training facility. The announcement has generated much local debate with regard to the perceived impact the development will have on the community of Wrexham.

Previous to this, in January 2012, Justice Secretary Chris Grayling committed to addressing the needs of military veterans; improving the level of support and rehabilitation available to them, in particular, to those who find the transition from the service to civilian life difficult and end up in the criminal justice system (Grayling, 2012).

This chapter provides a summary of a study which explored the opportunities for developing a community based social enterprise in Wrexham to support the needs of both ex-military offenders and the wider community. The study examined the effectiveness of social enterprise activity on recidivism rates, explored the needs of ex-military offenders, the local community and local economy. It did this through the use of a variety of research methods, including a literature review, interviews, case study analysis and site visits to similar projects, leading to the development and carrying out of a feasibility study into the delivery of a care farm / market garden social enterprise, which would provide work experience and training opportunities to meet identified market gaps, support community food growing initiatives and promote greater community integration.

The objective of the study was to demonstrate the scale of social enterprise activity within and around the prison service and its associated success in reducing reoffending levels and, with specific reference to the planned prison in Wrexham, to use this evidence to consider the feasibility of a new business.

Project Background

As a group of professionals working in specialist support provision throughout Wales, our services provide support to offenders upon their release from prison. With the news of this new prison being developed in Wrexham, we set out to identify if, in this setting, rehabilitation outcomes could be improved through provision of holistic support to assist offenders in their rehabilitation utilising social enterprise activity.

Initial research identified a specialist agency, already providing support to ex-military offenders in a nearby prison, which also has the experience and capacity to deliver social enterprise projects. Following this, and with a desire to develop an innovative social enterprise model, the study narrowed its focus to a specific target group of offenders, (ex-military offenders).

This led to identifying our vision as the development of a care farm, run by military veterans for ex-military offenders, which would enable them to access a range of support and interventions on release from prison. Through the provision of training and work experience in an agricultural and horticultural environment, the offenders would improve their personal wellbeing whilst developing skills and gaining qualifications with a view to fully integrating back into society and becoming work ready.

> *Care farming is defined as 'the use of commercial farms and agricultural landscapes as a base for promoting mental and physical health, through normal farming activity and is a growing movement to provide health, social or educational benefits through farming for a wide range of people* (Care Farms UK, 2014: 1)

The success of the proposed project will rely on the development of relationships and key alliances with partners and stakeholders including politicians, North Wales Probation Service, the local authority, veterans' societies, local communities, Care Farms UK, the prison management, training establishments and potential funders.

Project and Community Context

Strategic Policy Direction

Significant change is taking place in the UK's criminal justice system. The Ministry of Justice (2014) is introducing a reform programme, 'Transforming Rehabilitation', which will change the way offenders are managed in the community, in an attempt to reduce reoffending levels. Key aspects of it are:

- To create a new public sector National Probation Service to work with the most high-risk offenders and to form 21 new community rehabilitation companies (CRCs) to work with medium and low risk offenders;
- To give statutory supervision and rehabilitation in the community to every offender released from custody;
- To establish a nationwide 'through the prison gate' resettlement service to give most offenders continuity of support from custody into the community.

These changes will create opportunities for non-statutory organisations to deliver a range of services to support the management of offenders.

Wrexham is also experiencing significant change. It has a long history of association with the military services, having large barracks and being a principle employer in the area. Changes to national military strategy have led to recent structural changes as a result of 'Army 2020' (Ministry of Defence, 2014), which has seen a reduction in the military presence in the town and the economic activity associated with it. However, the long association is reflected in the increasing number of support organisations working to meet the needs of military veterans in the Wrexham area.[20] With the development of the new prison, Wrexham will need to develop services to support offenders upon their release.

While the variety of supports for military veterans in the town is substantial, however with the development of the new prison we have identified a looming gap in service provision with the development of the new prison. This is in relation to the rehabilitation of veterans who have been imprisoned and will be released from the new prison into the community. This study seeks to identify if this gap could be filled utilising the changes in offender management combined with social enterprise activity.

---

[20] Support organisations in the Wrexham area for military veterans and those on release from prison include: Combat Stress - mental health charity; Drug Intervention Programme; Salvation Army - housing issues; CAIS - Soup Dragon Service for the homeless; Royal British Legion; Alabare - provision of housing and employment opportunities.

Impact of Social Enterprise on Re-offending

There are an increasing number of social enterprises operating within the criminal justice system but there is limited knowledge of their impact on recidivism rates (Durham, 2011). In fact, despite increasing levels of social enterprise activity in the UK, reoffending rates are increasing with one in four criminals returning to crime within a year of release (Grierson, 2013). However, there is no evidence to link these two observations. In fact, it is argued that employment and enterprise are established and recognised factors that contribute to reduced levels of reoffending (Social Exclusion Unit, 2002). Indeed, it is contended that within the United Kingdom, high levels of recidivism are as a direct consequence of a lack of prison work opportunities (Shea, 2005).

It would seem that, while the correlation of social enterprise activity and reoffending rates may not be adequately measured, individual social enterprises *can* reduce and have a positive impact on lowering levels of reoffending. A report, 'Reducing reoffending through social enterprise' (Social Firms UK, 2009) attempted to quantify the scale and scope of social enterprise activity within prisons and probation services within England; identifying the positive and negative aspects of their involvement and identifying gaps in provision and models of good practice. This research showed that "social enterprises led to cost savings, provision of specialist expertise, creation of community links, ability to engage with hard to reach clients and innovation and creativity of service methods" (2009: 8).

In their 2010 review 'Barbed: What happened next?' The Howard League concludes that there are a number of factors which are critical to the success of work and social enterprise within prisons, notably – that prisons must ensure they provide a positive and supportive environment, work must be realistic, distinct from a prisoners living space and it is appropriate to work with external employers and allow the prisoner to experience realistic working conditions.

Needs of Ex-military Offenders

In exploring the specific needs of ex-military offenders, it was first necessary to develop an understanding of who they are. Research suggests that, although the proportion of ex-military personnel who offend is a small percentage of those discharged from the forces, there are significant differences between them and the general prison population in the nature of offending:

> *The average age of ex-servicemen in prison is older than the average of the general prison population... 25% of ex-servicemen are in prison for sexual offences compared to 11% of the civilian prison population... Ex-servicemen are also over-represented in offences categorised under the heading 'violence against the person' with some 32.9% being in prison for such offences, compared to 28.6% of the non-veteran prison population* (Howard League, 2011: 4).

The reasons why ex-military personnel find themselves caught up in the criminal justice system having left the armed forces was also considered and presented conflicting views. Despite a common public perception that a disproportionate number of individuals leaving the forces suffer with physical, emotional and mental health problems, in particular Post Traumatic Stress Disorder (PTSD), compared to the general population, Hurley states that there is little or no evidence to support this assertion. Indeed the presentation of mental health problems in this cohort is less than in the general population (Hurley, 2012). In contrast, The Howard League for Penal Reform independent enquiry (2009) into why ex-military personnel offend concluded that there were three main factors:

- The relevance of combat and associated effects of PTSD;
- The pre-forces background of service personnel (the forces commonly recruit from disadvantaged communities, often associated with crime. They offer a regular source of income structure and improved employment opportunities);
- The vulnerability of early service leavers (leaving, often suddenly due to disciplinary violations or through medical discharge and receiving minimal support for the transition back to civilian life).

In addition to those findings, the Howard Leagues report concludes that there is often a significant time lapse between discharge and imprisonment (approx. 10 years). This suggests that, while there is adequate support on discharge from prison (assistance in gaining employability skills, training, housing etc.), this is often time limited and not available later. But the support needs of ex-military personnel are multiple and complex can vary depending upon the reason for discharge and are not necessarily short-term.

Furthermore there is evidence to suggest that the needs of 'regular service leavers' are different to those 'medically discharged service leavers' or indeed 'early leavers' who are discharged as a result of drug/alcohol misuse, criminal acts, temperamental unsuitability or upon request to leave within four years. As a consequence this cohort can lose eligibility to resettlement entitlements (Nacro, 2010).

Overall, the literature considered in this study supported our perspective on the need for specialised support for ex-military offenders to assist their rehabilitation.

Developing a Feasibility Study

Having established a theoretical basis for provision of a specialist social enterprise support service for ex-military offenders, the process moved to developing and implementing a feasibility study. The study sought to test the feasibility of developing an agriculture and horticultural training provision for ex-military personnel within and upon release from Wrexham Prison. The continuity of support would be delivered through the training programme at the farm whilst continuing support would be provided by veteran support mentors.[21]

The feasibility study commenced with an assessment of current similar provisions through case study analysis, an exploration of the market demand for such a service and its products, identification and development of a suitable business model, the resources needed to deliver it and the tools for measuring its impact.

Case Study Analysis

A number of case studies of existing projects were identified and analysed under a series of key themes:
- Social enterprise activity within prisons;
- Social enterprise activity as part of rehabilitation process;
- Training and personal development of offenders;

---

[21] The client identified as most appropriate to further develop and implement this feasibility study was CAIS, North Wales' largest drug and alcohol charity. CAIS has extensive experience of supporting veterans as they currently lead on the delivery of the All Wales 'Change Step Programme' which is a mentoring and advice service delivered by veterans for veterans who are suffering from Post Traumatic Stress Disorder and other psychosocial problems.

- Support programmes for veterans.

The purpose of this thematic analysis was to assess the success of existing projects which share some of the characteristics of the proposed social enterprise and which combine the various elements of interest, namely:
- Provision of training in agriculture / horticulture within the prison (HMP Springhill, Farm and Garden Educational Centre);
- Provision of work experience in agriculture / horticulture on release from prison (HMP Winchester, partnering with the Forestry Commission and Willowdene Care Farm;
- Horticulture training programme being delivered through a social enterprise (Derwen Cornel Care Farm);
- Veterans Farm in the USA, which helps veterans over a 6 month programme rebuild their lives on leaving the services, by offering therapy through learning to farm, raising crops, working with animals and creating business plans (Veteransfarm, 2009).

Service Demand
In attempting to identify demand for the proposed service the study considered the following:
- Support for ex-offenders;
- Support for veterans;
- Skills gap in labour market.

Support for ex-offenders - research undertaken by Hine *et al.* (2008), refers to the pressure on health and social care providers as well as prisons and probation services to find solutions to tackle health and social care challenges such as prison overcrowding, re-offending rates and the increase in the number of disaffected young people (2008).

Support for veterans - In his report, 'Helping or Hindering Heroes', Hurley points out that the ex-military community amounts to around 4.8 million veterans and makes up 3.5 per cent of the UK prison population (2012). Translated to an expected population for Wrexham prison of 2100 prisoners, we calculate that at any one time there will be over 70 ex-military offenders incarcerated. Given that the average length of stay in this type of prison is just short of one year, there would be a demand to meet the support needs of this group.

UK Justice Secretary, Chris Grayling's articulated commitment to addressing the needs and improving the level of support and rehabilitation available to veterans who end up in prison to help them get their lives back together demonstrates a level of political support for specialist services to meet this client group's needs (Grayling, 2014).

<u>Skills gap in labour market</u> - Demand for the skills which this project would develop can be evidenced by a specific article on UK Agriculture's website which refers to the increasing age profile of farmers, many of whom are retiring without the traditional son/daughter wanting to take over the family business, thus leaving an industry with a skills shortage and declining workforce (2014).

Business Model
The business model being proposed is based on the award winning social enterprise *'Growing Well'* - a care farm providing training opportunities for individuals with mental health support needs, whose outcomes are consistent with the intended approach of this proposition.

The proposal is a social enterprise care farm / market garden which will provide a range of training and work experience opportunities in horticulture, agriculture and animal husbandry for up to ten ex-military offenders each year, on their release from Wrexham Prison. While it would be initially reliant on capital funding to develop the site, our budget proposals anticipate that the market garden business would become financially self-sustainable within five years.

A staged support model is proposed with offenders initially engaging with the mentoring programme provided whilst in custody, and then continuing to access mentoring and support around issues such as housing and benefits alongside the range of educational and work experience opportunities the social enterprise would offer.

A potentially suitable site has been identified and has been used as the basis for developing plans in consultation with an agricultural/horticultural expert, to identify crops and growing cycles that would maximise use of land and income generation.

Once developed, the site will accommodate a range of activities and training opportunities for the veterans and offenders including:
- Planting, maintaining and harvesting of crops and flowers;
- Caring for livestock and chickens and Bee keeping;
- Accredited qualifications in Level 1 Horticulture.

Working in partnership with the prison management, it is anticipated that the prison kitchens would become the primary customer for the produce. In addition to this it is planned that smaller crops would be sold through local farmers markets and other smaller businesses/social enterprises.

Building relationships with the local community is considered a key element of the project and will include allocating a portion of the land to the community for allotments; engaging with local gardening clubs; hosting competitions and holding an annual open day on site which showcases the work of the veterans. A market analysis and marketing strategy have also been produced and are available in the full report.

Resource Analysis
An analysis of our client's organisation (CAIS) identified extensive experience of working with veterans and individuals with complex needs; existing relationships with prospective stakeholders, experience of setting up and managing social enterprises and strong governance already in place. While the organisation has a lack of horticulture or agriculture experience, it is considered that it is nonetheless very well placed to develop this innovative concept further. The following resources have been identified as crucial to the project in order for it to do so.

Funding - It is envisaged that an element of both capital and revenue funding will be required for the set-up of the care farm and market garden.

Capital - Depending on the final site chosen we have estimated an initial grant of approximately £73,000 will be required to develop the land, buildings and purchase of equipment (figures calculated June 2014).

Revenue - funding for the first three years of the training programme will be required at an annual level of approximately £80,000 and it is suggested that the new provider of probation services be considered as a potential commissioner. Thereafter the level of revenue being created through the produce being sold is envisaged to contribute significantly and reduce the reliance on service level agreements (figures calculated June 2014).

Staffing - It is envisaged that a suitably qualified member of staff with relevant horticulture expertise will ultimately manage the site and be supported by a range of our client's staff (mentors, volunteer co-ordinator, project manager, and marketing staff). In addition to staff, the programme will be supported by volunteers, primarily from veteran societies and the local community.

Site - A potentially suitable site has been identified for the enterprise. If realised, this would provide a 12-acre piece of land (double the size of Growing Well's site). We understand that it is in public ownership and may be available for the project through a Community Asset Transfer scheme. Obtaining this or a similar site would significantly reduce any capital expenditure.

Impact Measurement
An impact measurement framework is essential for the proposed programme. The recommendation is to follow the *Seven Principles of Social Return on Investment* and NEF Consulting's Theory of Change (2014). Using these principles will ensure stakeholders (in this case the ex-military offenders) are involved throughout the process of planning, implementation, delivery and impact measurement of the programme.

A suggested measurement framework for the Care Farm / Market Garden would highlight external factors such as family, other supporting organisations and the outcomes that the stakeholders would deem important as a result of the programme. Key themes to include in impact measurement include social interaction, increased self-esteem and self-worth, education / training/ employment and a stable routine. Development of the framework should be a collaborative process, involving: interviews with the target group before, during and after the time spent at the farm, focus groups and interviews with volunteers and selected staff

This model's primary focus is on outcomes as opposed to outputs. Areas for consideration should include the client's goal setting, key themes emerging from the client's experiences and activities that are making an impact on the client's wellbeing. Outputs such as qualifications attained; number of participants completing a programme etc. will also be recorded. The activities recommended to assess the impact are as follows:

- Assessment of well-being of clients and volunteers (The Warwick-Edinburgh Mental Well-being Scale, Tennant *et al.*, 2007);
- Qualitative data collection that includes primary research (interviews) with clients;
- Secondary data (notes from supervision meetings from support staff).

Conclusion

This study has presented evidence to link social enterprise activity with positive impacts on re-offending levels and indicates that individuals who access care farms have enhanced mental health and well-being outcomes. The social enterprise care farm model is put forward to identify and address an unmet need, by providing opportunities for ex-military offenders to rehabilitate more effectively in a supportive and mentored, educational environment. The feasibility study has demonstrated that this model could meet the challenges which have arisen from the changes to the offender management process and the move towards wider community integration. In addition it supports community food growing, ex-offender physical and mental wellbeing and reductions in reoffending.

Finally, following the findings of the feasibility study, it is now intended to present the report to CAIS with a series of recommendations for development which will include: establishing a firm commitment to the initiative from partner agencies, conducting additional research and case study analysis of social enterprises providing care farm services specifically to ex-military personnel, preparing more detailed business plan with costs and implementation schedule.

Chapter 7
More than Housing: The Potential of the Housing Association Sector in Ireland to Use Social Enterprise Models to Contribute to Socio-Economic Development

Alan Curtis, Deirdre Whitfield, Margaret Cleary and Gerry Folan

Introduction

Social enterprise is about enterprise, about creating real and sustainable employment while yielding a social dividend which benefits communities including social housing communities. Social enterprise has yet to realise its full potential in an Irish context and can only do so to the extent to which an enabling environment is promoted.

Housing associations are, by definition, social enterprises which focus on the core business of quality social housing and reinvest any surplus towards promoting their social mission. While most are constituted as charities providing housing, they can identify with the principles and value base of social enterprise. In a new policy development, housing associations are being advanced by government to be at the centre of future social housing provision.

The austerity measures introduced as result of the economic downturn in Ireland and throughout Europe since 2008 have resulted in constraints on public expenditure which have impacted on a wide range of services, including social housing. This chapter focuses on the area of social enterprise and social housing and asks if voluntary housing associations can become drivers of social enterprise, where the housing association sector benefits from the delivery of enhanced services, and the social enterprise sector benefits from enhanced opportunities for development. This would represent an opportunity for reform, rather than for mere recovery, in this area. It would establish social enterprise as an important mechanism for socio-economic regeneration and social inclusion. At the same time, it would involve housing associations in providing more than just housing.

The chapter begins by framing this question within the context of current policy on social housing, social enterprise and social inclusion and argues that there is a synergy between these three sectors in that, firstly, they are all undergoing significant change in policy and practice and secondly, all three sectors come under the remit of the Department of Environment; Community and Local Government (DECLG). To date, there has been little primary research into the potential of housing associations and social enterprise to work together in an Irish context and this is the area which forms the focus of the research undertaken for this study.

The chapter concludes with a summary of the main discussions and the challenges facing housing associations and social enterprises in coming together to provide more than housing. It proposes an adapted or new model that would address the social and economic renewal of local communities beyond housing. In order to promote local economic and social development within communities, housing associations must have the capacity to deliver more than housing, either through creating, acquiring, facilitating or partnering with other social enterprises, and, also, most importantly with the support and endorsement of the Irish State.

Background

Social Housing
The conventional view of State involvement in the supply of social housing in Ireland has been challenged over the past number of years. Traditionally the model was one of State provision through local authorities. However, current housing policy is placing housing associations at the heart of housing provision (DECLG, 2011). With improved regulation and governance, the sector is expected to play a leading role in the future supply of housing, while still needing to leverage non-state capital investment.

This would involve changing the model for the provision of social housing from a bricks and mortar model to one of housing as a system 'where housing provision is understood as a network of interrelated organisational activities which both respond to and help to shape the changing social, economic, environmental, technological and political context in which housing bodies operate' (ENHR, 2013).

Social Enterprise
The concept of social enterprise has been part of the discourse of economic and social development for some time. According to the OECD, social enterprises have proven themselves to be able to

reduce social exclusion by reintegrating groups into the labour market; delivering services to marginalized groups; creating jobs at local level and increasing social capital and citizen participation (Noya, 2009). However, in the Irish context, there is a widespread acknowledgement that there is a lack of focused development of the social enterprise sector in general, and a lack of policy focus and direction at national level. In contrast, in Europe the social enterprise sector accounts for between 4 per cent and 7 per cent of GDP. In Ireland it represents just 3 per cent of GDP (SEETF, 2010). This means that Ireland still has the capacity for growth in the sector. It is estimated that it can generate an additional 5,000 jobs per annum over the next five years (Clann Credo, 2011). Furthermore, data taken from the Community Service Programme (CSP) review of a sample of 134 projects shows that social enterprises have the capacity to create additional finance (for every €1 from the Department of Social Protection (DSP) they generated a further €1.27 from traded/earned income) that produces a multiplier effect which has the capacity to generate local employment.

Recent developments appear to be addressing the gaps in policy. Following the publication of a report on social enterprise in Ireland (see Forfás, 2013) the Minister with responsibility for developing social enterprise has set up an inter-department committee to establish appropriate institutional oversight and co-ordination mechanisms for the sector, including assigning lead responsibility for social enterprise policy to the DECLG.

Social Inclusion
The DECLG is responsible for the successor to the Local Community Development Programme (LCDP) to be known as the Social Inclusion Community Activation Programme (SICAP). SICAP is a local social inclusion programme focused on the most marginalised in Irish society. It aims to tackle poverty and social exclusion through local engagement and partnership between disadvantaged individuals, community organisations and public sector agencies, and to operate across Ireland. SICAP has three goals with social enterprise specifically targeted in goal 3:

> To engage with marginalised target groups/individuals and residents of disadvantaged communities who are unemployed but

*who do not fall within mainstream employment service provision, or who are referred to SICAP, to move them closer to the labour market and improve work readiness, and support them in accessing employment and self-employment and creating **social enterprise** opportunities* (CWC, 2014: 8).

Thus it appears that this is an opportune time for increased co-operation between housing associations and social enterprise in order to maximise opportunities for addressing the socio-economic needs of social housing communities. This would involve a number of stakeholders, including the DECLG, who could achieve a number of objectives across different sections of the Department if the connections between these sections are acknowledged. Housing associations are among the other key stakeholders in this proposition. The next section focuses mainly on this sector.

Research and Findings
The methodology used to achieve the objectives of this study consisted of both primary and secondary research, using both quantitative and qualitative methods. The primary research comprised of a survey of a random sample of 66 groups, taken from the membership list of the Irish Council for Social Housing (ICSH). These represented both large and small organisations operating in both urban and rural areas. There were 34 valid responses which is equivalent to a response rate of 51.5 per cent. In addition, a series of semi-structured interviews were conducted with thirteen key informants involved in the policy area and operational side of the provision of social housing. Secondary research involved documentary analysis of academic sources and government policy papers on social enterprise, social housing and social inclusion.

The Housing Association Sector in Ireland
The majority of housing associations in Ireland are small in nature (one off developments) and set up to deal with specific disadvantaged groups such as people with disabilities; people who are homeless; older people and women who suffer from domestic violence. Table 5 below shows that there are 265 members of ICSH currently providing social housing unitswith just 38 (14 per cent) of these providing housing for general need. Of the 38, 11 (29 per cent) provide housing in more than

one county. The vast majority, 227 (86 per cent) of providers of social housing are dealing with specific target groups.

Table 5: ICSH Membership by Housing Provision Type

Service	Number	Percentage	Multi county by number	Multi county %
Domestic violence	11	4	0	0
Elderly only	102	38	1	1
Elderly and others	18	7	0	0
General	38	14	11	29
Homeless	35	13	4	11
People with Disabilities	60	23	7	12
Un-coded	1	0	0	0
Total	265	100	23	9

Housing Associations and Social Enterprise
Housing associations can be said to be a social enterprise because they are similar in nature and they share the following defining characteristics:
• The assets of the organisation are applied solely towards its social objectives (prime objective being the provision of housing need or the alleviation of poverty etc.);
• It generates income by selling and providing a service (housing accommodation) i.e. trade is the major and continuous activity;
• It reinvests its surplus into the organisation to fulfil its social objectives.

This study found that there is significant confusion in relation to what defines a social enterprise. This was very evident in the differences in responses to the survey and the interviews. In the survey the majority of respondents identified their organisational structure as charities with only two per cent of housing associations identifying their as social enterprises. This may be reflective of the importance attached to legal structure and tax designation by NGOs generally.

On the other hand, of 13 interviewees who were asked if they thought housing associations were social enterprises, 12 responded that they believed they were. One of the largest housing associations owns and manages circa 5,343 units with an annual turnover of €13.7m and identifies itself as a social enterprise, 'As an approved housing body

Cluid is a social enterprise and all of our surplus is reinvested in our business' (Cluid Housing Association, 2013: 55). One CEO acknowledged that as a large housing association 'We decidedly place ourselves in that role of being a social enterprise, a social business which delivers social wellbeing but our core business is housing which we need to ensure is sustainable before can move to the next level' (interview).

Table 6: Legal Structure of Social Housing Providers

Org. Type	Number	%
Social enterprise	2	7.5
Charity	20	74
Community Association	2	7.5
Private business	0	0.0
Other	3	11
Total Respondents	27	100

A number of interviewees also felt that not all housing associations would view themselves as social enterprises but rather as charities that come from a community base and work to provide social inclusion in the first instance. One such interviewee expressed why he thought his organisation was not a social enterprise as follows:

No, I wouldn't regard our organisation as a social enterprise because we employ about 170 staff and we receive 78% of government funding. The rest of it comes through rents and investments and stuff like that....I think a social enterprise in its truer sense needs to be able to financially stack up in its own right and because of our dependence on government funding I don't think you could regard it as a social enterprise.

These findings are indicative of that fact that, on the whole in Ireland, there is a general lack of understanding of social enterprise within the community and voluntary sector. For example, in a study of the CSP Programme which operates a social enterprise model, only 44 per cent of organisations surveyed considered themselves to be social enterprises (Curtis, 2010; Doyle and Lalor, 2012). However, among the interviewees in this study, there was a level of understanding of their organisation as a social enterprise and a level of identification with social enterprises. This was generally in terms of their role in housing provision.

The Potential of Housing Associations to Develop a Sustainable Social Enterprise Model

When asked, 78 per cent of organisations surveyed and all housing association representatives interviewed confirmed that they currently provide more than housing services. 87 per cent of survey respondents and all our key informants were positively disposed to housing associations delivering more than housing for the social and economic benefit of local communities. Many are already providing additional services to their tenants, particularly those that deal with to specific target groups or with people who have particular needs e.g. homeless people, people with disabilities. However, as much as respondents said that they could provide other services, it was also the case that access to resources was cited as a major obstacle in this regard. One interviewee noted 'The biggest challenge is the vast majority are very small scale and tend to be very dispersed geographically so getting it to stack up is a massive challenge'.

In terms of organisational resources, it is noteworthy that the smaller housing associations rely on either local Community Employment (CE) schemes or some other activation programmes. In addition, local people who were unemployed benefitted by participation on CE and Community Work Placement (TÚS) schemes. For example, a small housing association in Kildare relied on a combination of these schemes and volunteers to help keep the organisation afloat and to provide the additional services. One interviewee stated: 'We would require support from the state to provide the services'.

78 per cent of survey respondents indicated that they would consider developing a new social enterprise or partnering with an existing one. While this is encouraging, many of them also identified barriers to engaging with social enterprise including staff time and resources, and lack of business acumen. In addition they cited the difficulties with a national policy that focuses only on housing and on the financial and governance aspects of the housing associations. 30 per cent of respondents indicated that they had plans to operate as a social enterprise. The areas under consideration were:

- A community hub, which would include a café, garden centre or training facility;
- Access, advisory and support services;
- Employment opportunities;
- Bakery and farm;
- Training, construction and recycling.

The issue of well-being and community came up in the interviews in that many housing associations were cognisant of the need to be wary of falling into the trap that once housing is provided, their job is done.

Capacity

Overall the housing association sector manages 27,000 housing units nationally which equate to the total housing stock of Dublin City Council, the biggest local authority in the country. However with only 14 per cent of providers meeting general housing needs, and only 29 per cent of these operating outside county level, there are a limited number of housing associations which could deliver or manage housing in urban areas at a scale to meet the objective of creating real and sustainable employment while yielding a social dividend. For example, three out of five respondents from the smaller housing associations stated that it was not their job to provide employment for their residents. Two of them were providing specific services to homeless and people with disabilities and saw it as being outside of their remit. The other two respondents were much more open to the housing association providing employment and training but they said they were a long way off providing this as they did not have the scale and resources to develop further.

It would seem that capacity is limited to those who:
- Can engage in significant development at urban level through stock transfer or other means;
- Have potential to deliver more than housing with social enterprise mind-set;
- Can generate significant social impact.

The study findings show that it is difficult for the smaller housing associations to become involved in the provision of employment, training and other entrepreneurial activities, given that they are there to focus on their core service i.e. provision of housing needs. Focus on core business is also a priority for larger association such as Cluid who have three regeneration projects Killarney Court in Dublin, St. Patricks in Ballina and St. Michaels in Longford. According to the Chairperson they have worked quite well but they come at a price.

Scale

Housing associations have the potential to 'become catalysts for change' according to one interviewee, but in line with the views of others, he conceded that housing associations need scale to move beyond housing so as to support the economic and social needs of their communities and this is seen as a challenge by the vast majority of the providers of social housing.

Representatives of the smaller housing associations see the benefit of housing stock transfer, but they are adamant that this must be accompanied by 'resources and support'. There is agreement 'that smaller housing associations are being paralysed by bureaucratic processes, a lack of political clarity, inflexible rules and regulations, restrictive public procurement and the requirement to compete on purely financial grounds for contracts for the purchase of land to support their expansion.

One interviewee observed that 'there is significant opportunity for European Investment Bank funding in refurbishing stock that can only take place with substantial stock transfer to housing associations' but stresses that political ambiguity threatens investment.

It seems that creating social impact would require a project of significant scale with housing associations engaged in stock transfer, as part of a renewal or regeneration programme of local authority housing. Such an undertaking would require a joint venture approach by two major housing associations and/or with an experienced partner in housing and social enterprise from another country such as the United Kingdom. It would also require substantial funding from the European Investment Bank, leveraged on assets held by the housing associations, through stock transfer and a supportive national policy.

As noted by NESC (2014), such a proposal would unlock new funding for housing without adding to general government deficit or debt and create the use of newly generated capital to refurbish dwellings, improving their quality and returning derelict properties to occupation. The management and ownership of the properties would rest with housing associations, who would become the landlords of existing and new tenants. The potential for social enterprise to spin off such a development and deliver significant social impact in the designated areas would create a genuine opportunity for a housing led social enterprise approach.

Policy

The evidence suggests there is a need for clarity, direction and coherence of policy at state level which could shape a social enterprise agenda and create a stronger connection between social enterprise and housing policy. Building greater potential for social impact around housing provision through social enterprise is acknowledged by respondents as a desirable objective but is constrained by the absence of policy direction and supports. If government policy is serious about social cohesion, inclusion, and integration within communities it is suggested a more integrated approach is required.

Procurement

A number of the larger housing associations and the Minister with responsibility for housing have spoken about the possibility of incorporating a 'social clause' into any regeneration or transfer of local authority housing stock as part of a regeneration project. This would unlock the potential for housing associations to support social enterprise along the value chain.

Positive indicators are that 2013 saw the introduction of the "Social Clauses in Public Procurement Bill"[22] and the Minister noted that Limerick regeneration had included social clauses which could be used as a model.

Model for Addressing the Social and Economic Renewal of Local Communities Beyond Housing

The proposed model for development focuses on what might have the best chance of being sustainable if all the variables come together. It is focused on the larger housing associations and based on a convergence

---

[22] The Social Clauses in Public Procurement Bill, 2013 provides for the inclusion of social clauses in all public procurement contracts over €1 million, to provide opportunities for unemployed persons and apprentices, to ensure equality in the workplace in the carrying out of public contracts and to provide for sustainable development. It received an unopposed second stage reading in Dáil Éireann on 17th October 2014.

of policy within a single government department, the DECLG that has responsibility for local government, community and social enterprise and social housing. The DECLG can develop policy across, and within the relevant units (local government, housing and community) that would see the larger housing associations receive transfer of local authority housing stock as part of management or regeneration schemes and, in return, the housing associations would be required to develop a social clause that would see them support and develop local social enterprises in collaboration with the Local Community Development Committees (LCDCs) and local implementation bodies that will be managing the new Social Inclusion Community Activation Programme (SICAP). Housing associations can help unlock the potential of social enterprise by investing some of their income from their capital assets through stock transfer. Social enterprises set up by housing associations in the United Kingdom for example, are most commonly funded from reserves in the first instance. Many also use a mixture of grants, loans and investment from a variety of other sources.[23]

Adopting this model would mean that both the housing associations and the social enterprise sector would be in a position to attain some of their social objectives by providing services for their target groups and tenants to address social exclusion and contribute to local economic sustainability. It has the potential to address levels of unemployment, create greater social capital, and develop partnerships and collaborations that have not happened to any degree heretofore.

Housing associations could for example, partner with existing social enterprises, develop a social enterprise internally or collaborate with other bodies to develop social enterprises that could be stand alone and would leave the housing association to concentrate on what they do best and that is the provision of housing.

Conclusion

While there is confusion around the concept of social enterprise, a significant number of respondents believe housing associations to be social enterprises, demonstrating a level of awareness of the concept among Housing associations. Most of the housing associations would like to engage with social enterprise to deliver services but there are

---

[23] For a comprehensive report on these models see Social Impact Consulting's 'Green Light – Creating Jobs through Social Enterprise (2012).

concerns, which include drift from core mission, lack of resources and fears around capacity. There are replicable models from the United Kingdom, given a more advanced policy and support context in Ireland. Capacity however would be limited to those housing associations of sufficient scale to engage in stock transfer, which would enable them to leverage non-state funding and use income to either partner with, support or start up social enterprises to deliver more than housing. In addition, housing associations should be encouraged to use procurement processes to support social enterprise.

At a national level engagement with a social enterprise model will be dependent on a more holistic approach by Government departments and the involvement of LCDCs at county level. The experience of the financial crisis and the impact of austerity have led to a policy review of social housing, a renewed interest in social enterprise and a sharper focus on socio-economic development. A housing-led social enterprise approach can create new investment, thus rebuilding social capital and value in communities through greater inclusion and meeting social needs. This would be in line with the stated aims of local and national government, of promoting local economic and social development.

CHAPTER 8
THE POTENTIAL OF SOCIAL ENTERPRISES TO SUPPORT PEOPLE WITH INTELLECTUAL DISABILITIES TO OVERCOME BARRIERS TO EMPLOYMENT

Maighréad Kelly

> *People with intellectual disabilities have existed throughout our world across human history and make up a part of all cultures, they represent a small section of the extremely wide variety of people in the human population at any one time, yet they are still the most discriminated and stigmatised section of our society and are often the last within the community of disabled persons to receive attention* (Paramenter, 2011:2).

Introduction

People with intellectual disabilities are 'able to' and 'want to' work but cannot because of the barriers that they face. According to the Central Statistics Office (CSO) 2011 Census there are over 57,000 people with an intellectual disability in Ireland. Over 36 per cent of those aged between 15 and 65 years of age are in the labour force. According to the CSO, the most common difficulty experienced by those with an intellectual disability is in working or attending school or college, which affected over 57 per cent or around 33,000 persons of this group' (CSO, 2012).

In recent years, there has been a lot of positivity around the value of social enterprises in Ireland and their ability to be able to provide employment to individuals who are at a distance from the labour market. In 2012 the HSE published 'New Directions - A review of HSE Day Services and Implementation Plan, 2012 – 2016'. The report makes reference to the view that social economy and commercial work activities could play a useful role in vocational rehabilitation and in the pathways approach to labour market inclusion, not only for people with disabilities, but for all those at a distance from the labour market. It indicates that there is requirement for policy-makers to examine the 'mainstream social enterprise/economy framework' and further states that 'in line with the disability strategy, social enterprises should be managed by the government department and agency with responsibility for active inclusion and employment' (2012: 150).

To date, there has been very little research completed on measuring the outcomes for those people with intellectual disabilities who are presently working in social economy enterprises in Ireland or abroad. This chapter outlines a summary of a research study, which was undertaken in July 2014, exploring the potential for social enterprises to be able to support people with intellectual disabilities to overcome the barriers to employment that they experience.

Findings from the literature and case studies show that our thinking on employment for people, regardless of their ability or disadvantage, must extend beyond the traditional and conventional opportunities which, to date, have been offered in the competitive market and which do not offer adequate accommodations and supports.

The research study which informed this chapter has demonstrated that social enterprises designed specifically to support people with intellectual disabilities have greater potential to support those employees to overcome the barriers to employment. The findings also warn of the dangers of establishing social enterprises which are nothing more than a modern version of the segregated sector of sheltered workshops and job enclaves.

Research Objectives of the Study
This research set out to address the questions of whether employment enterprises that have been established to operate under the social enterprise model have the potential to support people with intellectual disability to overcome barriers to employment. It considered two possible ways: directly, by providing employment to people with intellectual disabilities or indirectly, by providing work experience and training so that the individual can access employment elsewhere in the labour market.

The methodological approach adopted for this study was qualitative as it was felt that a quantitative approach would not satisfactorily portray the complexity of the employment and social enterprise sector. The methods used included a literature review of secondary research, six case studies, a series of semi-structured interviews, one face-to-face and seven by telephone. The six case studies selected had different aims but shared two common objectives: they were established to create employment opportunities for marginalised groups of people;

they are not-for-profit and all of the earnings are reinvested back into the enterprise. It is noteworthy that identifying enterprises in Ireland that operate under a social enterprise model was a particular challenge as the majority of not-for-profit enterprises in Ireland are unaware of what it is that defines a social enterprise.

Employment, Intellectual Disability and Social Enterprises

In the first instance I reviewed the existing literature with the initial focus on the barriers that certain groups of people in our society face when trying to access employment. This was followed by consideration of the literature on the emergence and development of social economy enterprises both in Ireland and abroad and finally an analysis of the material on the role of social enterprises in creating employment opportunities for marginalised groups.

The term 'social enterprise' proved quite difficult to define in the context of the Irish perspective as it has yet to receive a clear and universal definition. Therefore for the purposes of this research study, the UK Department of Trade and Industry's (2002) definition was chosen. It defined a social enterprise as "a business with primarily social objectives whose surpluses are principally reinvested for that purpose in the business or in the community, rather than being driven by the need to maximise profit for shareholders or owners" (Doyle and Lalor, 2012: 9). The term 'social enterprise' was used interchangeably with the term 'social economy' and 'social economy enterprises' in order to describe businesses that are trading to achieve social objectives (Amin, 2002; Pearce, 2009).

The barriers that people with intellectual disabilities experience when entering the work environment are often complex and require multi-stakeholder involvement. Typically these barriers can be categorised as either internal or external.

Internal barriers can include: a lack of motivation or self-confidence, inadequate work experience, low levels of literacy and numeracy, the presence of challenging behaviour, and difficulties understanding unwritten workplace rules (Jahoda *et al.*, 2008 (cited in Trembath *et al.*, 2010); Shier *et al.*, 2009; Winn amd Hay, 2009; Lemaire and Mallik, 2008; Martorell *et al.*, 2008).

External barriers which may have a negative impact can often include: a lack of job opportunities, lack of appropriate support, and discrimination and stigmatization in the workplace (Grant, 2008; Shier *et al.*, 2009; Butcher and Wilton, 2008; Winn and Hay, 2009 cited in Trembath *et al.*, 2010).

Despite extensive research into what needs to occur in order for people with intellectual disabilities to successfully transition to employment, the evidence suggests that the current system, whilst effective for some, is not working. People with intellectual disabilities require specific support on each step of the journey and it does not end once the person has been employed.

Why Social Enterprise?

Social enterprises are businesses that are established, within the social economy, in order to address social inclusion on a broad scale in a cost effective manner. Examples include labour market activation, education and training provision, transport provision, housing development, environmental services, social care and childcare. They do this through meeting the needs of specific interest groups, for example, people with a disability. They identify the social need and address it in manner that is innovative, tackle social issues such as inequality and exclusion and build social capital in order to remain sustainable (Clarke and Eustace, 2009).

Social enterprises are run in the commercial sphere and operate under the traditional business model but unlike private for profit enterprises their sole objective for making a profit is to address a social need. A 2009 study by Clarke and Eustace identified that social enterprises build social capital, provide value for money, and have innovative solutions to problems. They are self-sufficient and are governed by a group of people who don't make a profit from the enterprise. Social enterprises have the capacity to provide jobs across a range of skill-sets and to provide employment to those most distant from the labour market, both spatially and socially. The study also showed that "from an economic perspective social enterprise builds community assets and engages in new economic activity that might not otherwise happen" (Clarke and Eustace, 2009: 60).

Social Enterprises that Create Employment Opportunities for Marginalised Groups

Shahmash (2010) asserts that traditional employment models do not provide inclusive support to those who face multiple, persistent barriers and that this is due to the fact that they don't have the resources or experience to be able to accommodate the specialised needs of these employees. This reduces the opportunity for the individual to participate in the work place which excludes them even further. Aspects of the traditional model that can contribute to exclusion include the hiring process, training environment, specific job tasks and prerequisites for job retention.

Over the last number of years a number of social enterprises have been established to provide a new employment model. In these situations the social programme is the business and its mission centres on creating employment opportunities for its target group. This group will consist of people who encounter significant barriers to employment and will typically include the homeless, people with disabilities, , at-risk youth and ex-offenders.

These organisations will often operate an enterprise which sells a product or a service to the open market, while employing people from its target group. The type of business will be predicated on the scope and appropriateness of the employment it creates for its target group. This includes skills development, consistency with their capabilities and limitations, as well as the commercial viability of the business.

The organisations will often offer social support services for their employees or trainees, which can include 'job coaching', 'soft skills training' and 'counselling'. The social enterprise aims to achieve financial self-sufficiency through the sales of its products and services, with the income used to pay the operating costs which are associated with the business. The profits also go towards paying additional social costs required to support those from its target group (Alter, 2007).

People with Intellectual Disabilities within the Social Enterprise Sector
According to Lysaght in her 2010 editorial piece in the Journal for Intellectual Disabilities, the real goal of inclusive employment is to enable people with intellectual disabilities to find meaningful work which will optimise their own productive capacities, will enable growth and development and will be rewarding and satisfying for the individual.

Research has shown us that community-based employment contributes to quality of life, autonomy and psychological health (Lysaght, 2010; Johoda *et al.*, 2008). This is particularly the case with social enterprises that have emerged as a form of community-based employment, offer both training and employment and are formed to directly address social needs through their products or services or through the numbers of disadvantaged people that they employ (Lysaght, 2010; Boschee *et al.*, 2010).

According to Katz and Kauder (2011) it has been their experience in the Kessler Foundation in Canada that social enterprise businesses are a viable strategy for creating good, meaningful employment. But why would this be the case? According to Ancheier and Seibel (cited in Amin *et al.*, 2003) third sector organisations, which is where social enterprises are placed, are 'better able to cope with the economics of specialised provision...' which is further supported by Amin *et al.* when they state that social enterprises' 'commitment to combating social exclusion is said to give them a unique understanding of what it takes to help individuals to become active economic agents and citizens' (Amin *et al.*, 2003: 6).

Social enterprises which have been specifically designed to create jobs for people with disabilities or other people that are disadvantaged are often referred to as the modern development of the sheltered employment models. A number of countries have developed these new models, examples of which are Social Firms in the UK and Affirmative Businesses in the US (Boschee *et al.*, 2010). The National Disability Authority stated in their 2010 research series that these:

New forms of social enterprise models are promising. They take on board ideas around social and financial inclusion - employing both people with and without disabilities in real jobs - and the idea of the broader social enterprise movement - that it is possible to use self-financing business structures and methods to achieve social benefits (NDA, 2010: 91).

Paramenter (2011) notes that there needs to be further research on the outcomes achieved by these forms of enterprises and cites Forester-Jones *et al.*'s study which was completed in 2010 and involved comparing forty people working in a social enterprise and forty others who were attending day centres. The study demonstrated that those who were working in the social enterprise scored higher on measures of life experience, self-esteem and satisfaction and concluded that social enterprises represent better training for future employment compared to day centres but that, even in those environments, social inclusion was inadequate. In this context, Katz and Kaunder (2011) identified a number of 'thorny issues' in relation to social enterprises and people with intellectual disabilities which, in their opinion, alienate many progressive thinkers who are committed to increasing integrated, community employment for people with disabilities. These issues include:

- The existence of sheltered workshops or enclaves within the social economy, whereby people with disabilities continue to be segregated from the open labour market and do not work alongside others who do not have a disability;
- The existence of sub-minimum wages or training allowances whereby people are working alongside people who don't have a disability and are not receiving proper payment for the work.

Parallel to this the social enterprise itself needs to be run as a true business; otherwise it will not be in a position to compete in the open market. Therefore it needs to have a robust business model, be managed by people who have solid experience of operating a business, have the capability to measure success and strive towards being financially sustainable (Katz and Kaunder, 2011).

Further research carried out in Canada found that social enterprises that have combined their extensive knowledge of disability, its impact and its required accommodation with business knowledge and expertise, are better placed to provide effective and supportive employment opportunities. People with intellectual disabilities require ongoing 'repetitive' training and the workplace needs to be innovative in order to have the necessary supports in place to provide the individual with intensive training, job coaching and support (Lemon and Lemon, 2003, cited in Broad and Saunders, 2008).

Summary of the Findings from the Case Studies

As described earlier, a case study approach was taken which firstly identified a sample of social enterprises in Ireland and Wales supporting people with intellectual disabilities to overcome barriers to employment. The following enterprises were identified:

Table 7: Social enterprises working in the area of intellectual disability

Smiles Newsagents, Dublin	Smiles Newsagents provides employment to people with and without disabilities, including people with intellectual disabilities. Training is providing on the job.
The Delta Centre, Carlow	The Delta Centre provides employment, work experience, vocational training, and operates a supported employment programme in Carlow for people with intellectual disabilities.
Hand on Heart Enterprises, Dublin	Hand on Heart Enterprises provides work experience on the Tus Initiative and on the job training to people with disabilities.
Dolmen Rainbow Cleaners Limited, Mayo	Dolmen Rainbow provides employment to people who are disadvantaged or marginalised, including people with intellectual disabilities. Training is provided on the job.
Speedpak, Dublin	Speedpak provides work experience and training for all people who experience a disadvantage.
Porters Coffee Shop and Bistro, Colwyn Bay, Wales	Porter's provides work experience and training to people who are disadvantaged.

Significantly, the research showed that Ireland has a broad and varied range of employment related services for people with disabilities within the social economy but only a very small number are categorised as operating under the social enterprise model. This could be attributed to the fact that there is no clear definition around what constitutes a social enterprise. The research and study of the enterprises that are operating within the social economy setting demonstrated that they have emerged largely due to a lack of opportunity for people to access employment in the wider private and public sector. According to the Health Research Board (HRB) in their 2007 report these types of services are beginning to grow in an ad-hoc fashion similar to the development of sheltered workshops over twenty years ago (HRB, 2007).

A sheltered workshop involved large numbers of people with varying degrees of intellectual disabilities carrying out contract work in workshops specifically established for that purpose. They typically worked in poor conditions, received very little support and had little interaction. People working in sheltered workshops retained their social welfare benefits, typically disability allowance, and would usually receive a small discretionary additional weekly payment from the work provider (National Rehabilitation Board, 1997).

This study demonstrated that despite a lot of positive change in attitudes to people with intellectual disabilities and the introduction of disability and equality legislation, people who have an intellectual disability continue to experience persistent and significant barriers to employment, a situation which is not unique to Ireland. The literature on social enterprise has demonstrated that enterprises which have been created to provide employment opportunities for marginalised groups do have the potential to support people with intellectual disabilities. However, the findings of the case studies have demonstrated that social enterprises which have been established within the disability sector have greater potential than those that have been established for the sector in general as they have the knowledge and experience of working with people who have specific support requirements.

Taking what Katz and Kaunders (2011) outline as the four characteristics which need to be present in a successful social enterprise, the following was found:

- People with disabilities working in integrated community jobs along-side people who don't have a disability - *All of the enterprises that studied were providing employment and / or work experience for people with and without a disability in local communities;*
- Individuals with disabilities are paid at least minimum wage or higher (market rate) - *Three of the six enterprises employed and paid people above the minimum wage;*
- Individuals with disabilities have a choice in deciding where they work - *All of the employees that were employed chose to apply to work there and went through an interview alongside other people who did not have a disability;*
- Regular skill assessment and the opportunity for advancement is present for all employees - *All of the enterprises provided ongoing skill assessment and training in order to advance either within or outside of the enterprise.*

Discussion

Some would argue that it is society that is the main barrier to inclusive employment for people and, even though research has shown that employers are positive towards employing people with a disability, the world of employment is still stigmatising them (Burge *et al.*, 2007). This includes perceptions of incompetence, social inadequacy and the belief that all people with disabilities have extensive needs (Kirsh *et al.*, 2009). In order for employment to be successful for a person with an intellectual disability there needs to be back up support and where there is no support it is almost inevitable that the employment relationship will breakdown (Burge *et al.*, 2007).

Research has shown that the current system of supported employment is not adequate and is only supporting a small minority of people with intellectual disabilities in the work place. The Irish Association of Supported Employment (IASE), in its submission to the employment strategy 2014, states that there should be provision for:

> *...long-term supports to both the individual with a disability and employer as appropriate and as required by them. These supports can be provided by a trained job coach with the backup of a professional supported employment service. This must be assessed based on each individuals needs and tailored to their employment needs. Long term means long term as necessary* (IASE, 2014: 4).

The failure of the current supported employment programme is one of the reasons why all of the enterprises that were studied were developed; it was out of the need for employment opportunities for particular groups of people who face multiple and persistent barriers to employment. The enterprises also indicated that, where possible, they support employees to access paid employment in the wider labour market but this is happening less and less. Research has shown that the workplace and paid employment have been dramatically impacted by 'global economic restructuring' which has resulted in, as Torjman (2002) calls it, the 'survival of the fittest' approach to public policy (Broad and Saunders, 2008). According to Dowse (2009) this presents further barriers for people to access employment and raises questions about the reality of people with intellectual disabilities gaining paid employment in the mainstream labour market.

Establishing a social enterprise is not easy; both the case studies and review of previous research has demonstrated that setting up an enterprise takes times and requires a lot of revenue. The study further shows that there are very few social enterprises with a remit to provide employment for people with intellectual disabilities, who are profitable and do not rely on additional support and funding.

It is clear that our thinking on employment for people, regardless of their ability or disadvantage, must extend beyond the traditional and conventional opportunities which to date been offered in the competitive market and which do not offer adequate accommodations and supports. We need to also think beyond the segregated sector of sheltered workshops and job enclaves. Research to date, whilst limited, has shown that consumer-run businesses, community-based non-profits and local social enterprises are places where people can develop their human capacity and function as 'co-operative producers of the market means of life' (Macpherson, 1985; Quarter and Ryan, 2010; Vaillancourt and Tremblay, 2002 cited in Prince, 2014).

Recommendations

While this research has indicated that there is potential to achieve positive outcomes for people with intellectual disabilities employed in social enterprises but there is also a need for more action. In light of that the chapter make the following recommendations:

- There is a need for a clear definition around the terms 'Social Enterprise' and 'Social Economy Enterprises' which were used interchangeably throughout the research;
- There needs to be an open, honest discussion between public agencies and civil society about what is and is not possible when it comes to developing social enterprises which seek to employ people who are disadvantaged;
- In order to avoid the risk of producing more sheltered workshops or other forms of employment enclaves, enterprises that are currently providing employment to people with intellectual disabilities need to consistently question their motives and ask themselves the following:
  - What do our enterprise activities say about disability?
  - Do our actions provide inclusive spaces and positive images around disability and diversity, or are we just reproducing traditional attitudes and barriers?

- In line with the views of Katz and Kauder (2011), all non-profit organisations considering creating a social enterprise business employing people with disabilities must ask themselves some hard questions prior to establishing the enterprise:
  - What is the purpose in starting a business?
  - What kind of business aligns with our mission?
  - Is our organisation's culture ready for change?
  - What is the level of risk our organisation is willing to take?
  - Does the organisation have access to capital or resources to invest in the start-up?

It is clear that our approach to creating meaningful employment opportunities for people, regardless of their ability or disadvantage, must extend beyond the traditional and conventional efforts which to date been offered in the competitive market and which do not offer adequate accommodations and supports.

CHAPTER 9
COMMON ENTREPRENEURIAL TRAITS? - A STUDY OF THE LINK BETWEEN SOCIAL ENTREPRENEURS AND FAMILY BUSINESS ENTREPRENEURS IN IRELAND

Michelle Daly-Hayes

Introduction
The idea that entrepreneurship is a distinct area of study has been established since the early nineteenth century. It has roots in the areas of psychology and economics and is yet separate again from business, economics or management studies. The perception that an entrepreneur is essentially 'born not made' is still a popular concept within most of the academic literature (Shefsky, 1994; Flora, 2006). This research was undertaken to explore more fully the psychology and nature of entrepreneurship, with particular reference to the areas of social and family business entrepreneurship.

Today there is a new emphasis on the study and development of entrepreneurial skills and in supporting individuals to acquire the skills needed to establish successful businesses and organisations. While undoubtedly, there are variations in psychological make-up and characteristics of entrepreneurs across the spectrum, what this research set out to investigate was the level commonality of traits and characteristics between family business entrepreneurs and social entrepreneurs. The study examined the traits and attitudes attributed (or identified as common) to both social entrepreneurs and family business entrepreneurs with the core research question being: 'Are there common traits or characteristics between social entrepreneurs and family business entrepreneurs?'

Background

Why are Social Entrepreneurs Important in an Irish Context?
The role of social enterprise in the overall economy is recognised as being important, particularly in the wake of the most recent recession (Katz and Page 2010). Internationally the role of social enterprise in supporting and developing economies has been well documented with researchers such as Austin *et al.* (2006) and Wickham (2006) noting the

strategic positive influence that social entrepreneurship has on commercial activity within an economy. In Ireland, a recent study by The Wheel (2014) looking at the non-profit sector in Ireland found that as the worldwide recession has progressed Ireland has seen more and more people become involved with, and respond to social enterprises than ever before. The establishment of a Social Enterprise Task Force in Ireland in 2011, led in part by Clann Credo to advocate social enterprise and social entrepreneurship as a viable and vibrant part of the Irish economy and society is one example of this dynamic.

Hynes examined the challenges and the issues with developing a social enterprise sector in modern post-recession Ireland. Successive Irish governments have aimed to promote entrepreneurship and implemented several programmes encouraging enterprise, for example a strong expansionist policy and the setting up of several quasi-state organisations, e.g. Enterprise Ireland, Local Enterprise Offices, Clann Credo, Ulster Community Investment Trust (UCIT) and others to develop this part of the sector for the past number of decades (2009).

Government policy as described by several Enterprise Ireland reports in the 1990s and 2000s was to "to promote the development of a strong internationally competitive enterprise sector in Ireland. (European Commission Structural Fund Grants, 1994: 1) this now includes social enterprise as a type of enterprise.

The role of social enterprise as a response to the most recent recession has been a well-documented phenomenon. Overall, social enterprises appear to be more active in comparison to commercial enterprises in launching new services or products (Seluis, 2011; Vujić, 2011)

Jayawarna (2010) has identified social enterprise as a potential strategic response to recession. The third sector has been growing despite the recession in other countries and could be a route to development and recovery also in Ireland. Social enterprise offers both the development of social capital and a future for community- led economic development. According to Clann Credo in Ireland in 2011, the social enterprise sector has the potential to develop to the level and scale that has been achieved in other countries: representing at least 5 per cent of GDP as well as contributing hugely to achieving the job creation goals set out by the Innovation Taskforce.

To realise this, Clann Credo and other national organisations involved in funding and supporting social enterprise suggest that, the sector needs an appropriate national policy framework (i.e. policy development located in the department with responsibility for enterprise), access to relevant support structures (i.e. SME support structures such as County Enterprise Boards, Enterprise Ireland, Business Innovation Centres, etc.) and most importantly access to capital. However, the social enterprise sector is seriously underdeveloped and its growth is hindered by a number of factors: a lack of policy focus and direction at national level; over-reliance on grant aid and limited access to other sources of finance; limited support structure and problems accessing the supports available to SMEs. A way of identifying and supporting new or potential social entrepreneurs would be most useful in the challenge of developing the sector in Ireland.

Forfás has found that the non-profit sector in Ireland, in its broadest sense, employs an estimated 100,000 people and has an income of over €6 billion. Within this, the social enterprise sector employs between 25,000 and 33,000 people in over 1,400 social enterprises, with a total income of around €1.4 billion (2013). This relates the importance of this burgeoning sector in Ireland today.

We are also told that The European Commission has placed the social economy and social innovation at the heart of its concerns under the Europe 2020 strategy. In 2011, the European Commission launched the Social Business Initiative as part of the Single Market Act within which social enterprise is one of 12 priority areas. Social enterprise accounts for about 6 per cent of GDP across the EU and the European Commission's 'Europe 2020' Strategy sets a target for this contribution to grow to 9 per cent of GDP over the decade to 2020.

Family Business Entrepreneurs and Social Enterprise
One type of successful business and a specific of this study is the family business and in particular the successful family business entrepreneur. Issues which influence family business longevity and success in Ireland are succession, business strategy, shareholding complexities and the trading environment. A study on profiling family businesses by Birdthistle and Fleming (2007) found that very few studies on family business have been conducted in Ireland despite the fact that there are approximately 200,000 Irish family businesses and it is estimated that

between 40 per cent and 50 per cent of the private sector workforce are employed in family-owned businesses (Hickie, 1995; Smiddy, 2002). In 2005, pre-recession, nearly half of all businesses in Ireland were family owned (CSO 2005), but this situation changed with the advent of the recession. According to research undertaken by BDO Simpson Xavier Accountants in 2006 two thirds of family owned businesses were expected to change ownership over the following ten year (Sheehy, 2006).

A survey by Price Waterhouse Coopers of family businesses in Ireland in 2012 found that: 'Family businesses in Ireland have performed relatively badly over the last year but are looking to grow over the next five years. 52 per cent have grown in the last 12 months (compared with 65 per cent globally) and 77 per cent are aiming to grow over the next five years (compared with 81 per cent globally)' (PWC, 2012: 3-4).

Both family businesses and social enterprises are elements of the rich tapestry that makes up the fabric of the Irish economy today. There is a very practical value in being able to understand the motivations and the characteristics that drive individuals to start-up businesses and to trying to encourage and develop those tendencies in future generations of social entrepreneurs and entrepreneurs.

Methodology
The methodological approach taken to meet the objectives of this study involved both primary and secondary research, using both quantitative and qualitative methods. The primary data collection method involved a survey which was distributed to various community groups, representative bodies and groups of entrepreneurs and social entrepreneurs. It was circulated online to 500 prospective respondents and had a response rate of 10 per cent. In addition to the survey a series of interviews were conducted to verify and support the quantitative data. Data collection was undertaken May-July 2014 with analysis being done during July-August 2014. The primary research was informed by a literature review involving academic sources and Government and statutory agencies policy papers and reports.

Main Findings of the Research

The results are presented under the methodological headings of survey and interviews. Interviews are analysed according to the six main characteristics of an entrepreneur as defined by Gartner (1990) and Lackeaus (2013).

Survey

Of the 50 respondents to the survey: 30 per cent identified themselves as social entrepreneurs; 14 per cent identified themselves as family business entrepreneurs; and 12 per cent identified themselves as other. Of the 12 per cent, when asked to clarify, the majority of those respondents were actually involved in social enterprise of one sort or another. The lack of a universally acknowledged definition of social enterprise is one reason suggested for this identity crisis within the sector.

Over 40 per cent of respondents had no volunteers within their organisations. This reflected the small size of most of the respondent organisations. Of the others, 34 per cent had less than ten volunteers; 14 per cent had more than 10 with only 12 per cent having more than 50.

The majority of survey respondents, 86 per cent, supported the view that, for the most part, the range of knowledge, skills and characteristics required for one to be a successful social entrepreneur and those to be a successful family business entrepreneur were similar. They identified and rated the primary characteristics as outlined below in Table 8. This supports one of the emerging themes of the overall research investigation that social entrepreneurs and family business entrepreneurs share common characteristics but differ in their motivations and applications.

Table 8: Most important characteristics identified by the respondents

Drive, Ambition, Need for Achievement	85%
Risk Appetite	37%
Intrapersonal Skills	48%

Other characteristics identified but given significantly less weight by the respondents were: locus of control; innovativeness; ambiguity tolerance; self-confidence.

Respondents were asked if they felt that entrepreneurs, either social entrepreneurs or family business entrepreneurs were born or made. The response to this was closely split with 51 per cent believing that entrepreneurs are made and 49 per cent believing that they are born.

Interviews

Following the survey a series of semi-structured interviews were conducted with a number of social entrepreneurs and family business entrepreneurs. The interviews focused on the characteristics considered necessary to be an entrepreneur and assessed them as criteria for success. The selection of characteristics was informed by the findings of the survey and supported by the work of Gartner (1990) and Lackeaus (2013) that attributed six specific characteristics to successful entrepreneurs – ambiguity tolerance; appetite for risk; locus of control; need for achievement; self-confidence; and innovativeness.

Ambiguity Tolerance

Ambiguity tolerance in the context of a social entrepreneur or family business entrepreneur is defined as 'the tendency to perceive ambiguous situations as desirable'. This was first defined as a discriminating variable between entrepreneurs and non-entrepreneurs by Schere (1982).

An ability to tolerate ambiguity was seen as a defining characteristic of social entrepreneurs and family business entrepreneurs by several of the interviewees who felt that they had a higher tolerance of ambiguity and that it was necessary in their work. The need to be able to deal with uncertainty or ambiguity was seen as being essential. One interviewee, a family business entrepreneur redefined it as *'not being afraid to fail or to do the unexpected or unfamiliar'*.

Appetite for Risk

Interviewees defined appetite for risk in the context of entrepreneurship as being the willingness to invest time and effort in a new development or a completely untried strategy or business. Risk appetite is more commonly described as the level of risk that a person or corporation is willing to take in order to execute a strategy. The social entrepreneurs and family business entrepreneurs interviewed all had a relatively high appetite for risk and felt that it was a core characteristic required by entrepreneurs like themselves.

It is important to note that any analysis of risk appetite within a group of individuals is very difficult due, primarily to its level of subjectivity. The level of risk that is tolerable for one individual may not be so for another.

Locus of Control

Psychologist Julian Rotter (1954) suggests that our behaviour is controlled by rewards and punishments, and that it is these consequences of our actions that determine our beliefs about the underlying causes for these actions.

> *A locus of control orientation is a belief about whether the outcomes of our actions are contingent on what we do (internal control orientation) or on events outside our personal control (external control orientation)* (Zimbardo *et al.*, 1985: 275).

The interviewees, both the social entrepreneurs and the family business entrepreneurs had a strong desire for locus of control and felt that this was a core characteristic required by entrepreneurs like themselves. They identified a desire to control the circumstances of their community and also felt that individual family circumstances played a major part in them establishing their organisations. As one interviewee family business entrepreneur put it:

> *Most of my friends at the time went into known safe secure jobs. They became doctors, lawyers, they began working in the civil service etc. But competitive business was my background so I never felt that any other option was for me.*

All of the interviewees had an awareness of their own need for control, the need to control their own destiny but the social entrepreneur interviewees showed a higher level of self-awareness. A social entrepreneur interviewee:

> *I don't think I could work for someone else; I've always wanted to work for myself. Creating my social enterprise has given me this opportunity.*

Need for Achievement

All of the interviewees, social entrepreneurs and family business entrepreneurs alike displayed a strong need for achievement and felt that this was a core characteristic required by entrepreneurs.

The interviews revealed important differences in the motivation and identification of achievement or success between the family business entrepreneurs and the social entrepreneurs. Family business entrepreneurs were largely motivated by desire to be more financially successful, to change their families' circumstances and to contribute socially or to community when they had achieved a level of financial success and status. The social entrepreneurs, on the other hand, were motivated by a desire to achieve for their community or their sector and not motivated by financial success to any extent.

While there were differences of opinion on what constituted achievement, both the social entrepreneurs and the family business entrepreneurs considered need for achievement a highly motivating factor. Both groups had clearly defined understandings of success and what achievement looked like in the context of their business or social enterprise. In the case of one social entrepreneur:

I had already set up and sold on a tech start up and it was with this experience that I approached creating a technology-based social enterprise.

His previous achievements in the commercial world had been in a family business. He believed that his commercial success in that business led to and added sense of confidence in the social enterprise sector.

Several of the interviewees considered that the prevalent attitude in the social sector in Ireland was one of scepticism of social enterprise and traded revenue within an organisation with a social purpose. Many also mentioned the tendency to rely on government funds and grants to sustain social businesses. One interviewee called it a *'sense of entitlement'* whereas a social enterprise in his opinion was one that was established like a regular business, where if a profit is not made or at least a loss prevented it is not going to exist.

Self-confidence

Bénabou and Tirole looked at the role of self confidence in the achievement of success. They analysed the value placed by rational agents on self-confidence, and the strategies employed in its pursuit. They found that confidence in one's abilities generally enhances motivation, making it a valuable asset for individuals with imperfect willpower (2002).

In the interviews time and time again all interviewees cited self-confidence, confidence and self-belief as necessary traits for the successful social entrepreneur or family business entrepreneur. One entrepreneur, BT mentioned that confidence was crucial to her setting up on her own in business: *"If I didn't believe in me, no one else would and failing was not an option."*

Often in descriptions of how they started their businesses the entrepreneurs described a critical point or a tipping point, beyond which they were unemployable or unwilling to work for other people. The need to succeed is based on the confident belief that the entrepreneur can change their own circumstances.

Innovativeness

Innovation is a key driver of change in businesses and organisations with business in general favouring the brave (or risk takers as previously discussed). In business, innovation often results when ideas are applied by the company in order to further satisfy the needs and expectations of the customers. In a social context, innovation helps create new methods for alliance creation, joint ventures, flexible work hours, and creation of buyers' purchasing power.

Innovativeness is the characteristic trait associated with someone who regularly approaches challenges and problems in their lives with a desire to solve them creatively. In interview, both the social entrepreneurs and the family business entrepreneurs indicated a talent for innovation and further suggested saw it as a core characteristic required by entrepreneurs. Innovation was one trait particularly associated with the social entrepreneurs who were, for the most part, seeking to address a societal problem through the creation of an organisation that would provide a sustainable solution.

However, innovation was seen as being essential in business also. Continuing to develop and delivering new services or products is an integral part of remaining in business. One family business entrepreneur stressed its importance and described it as differentiation, standing out from the competition by changing the process or changing what you are offering to the customer.

Conclusion

As can be seen, the main finding of this research study is that social entrepreneurs and family business entrepreneurs share common characteristics but differ in their motivations and applications. That is they share essential 'entrepreneurial DNA' but the output of their work is different and benefits different groups. The main characteristics identified as being shared by both sets of entrepreneurs were an ability to deal with uncertainty and indeed to revel in it; a willingness to take a risk in order to achieve a goal; a need to control their own destiny; a constant demand for reinforcement through identifiable achievement; high levels of self-belief; and an innovative approach to problem solving. A further finding is that a percentage of social entrepreneurs evolve in an organic sense from a family business entrepreneurial background.

It is hoped that a better understanding of these traits and the identification of definite links between the two types of entrepreneur in Ireland will contribute to better training and development. The focus of EU and Irish Government policy may place emphasis on the social sector of the economy as the recession recedes. In that context, this research could provide a starting point for further study into these two separate types of entrepreneur and add to the existing knowledge base.

Chapter 10
Brand Personality and Social Enterprises

Alison Hill

Introduction

Brand personality is an effective way of marketing an organisation, service or product. It is a particularly effective tool for social enterprises for two main reasons:

- Brand personality can communicate an organisation's values to consumers and social enterprises are essentially value driven entities. (Consumers are more likely to purchase products and services from organisations with which they share values).
- Unlike non-profit organisations' social enterprises embrace business practices and therefore should have less reticence or concerns about embracing branding on the basis of it being 'too commercial'.

In order to develop and manage its brand personality an organisation needs a mechanism (or instrument) to identify it. While such instruments have been developed in both the for-profit and the non-profit sectors, no instrument has been developed specifically for the social enterprise sector. Social enterprises are different to both for-profit and non-profit organisations, being a unique combination of the two. It therefore stands to reason that, in order to take full advantage of the business benefits that could accrue from developing and managing its brand personality, a social enterprise needs to have access to a brand personality instrument that is fit for purpose.

Defining Social Enterprise

Social enterprise has been described as a hybrid form composed of elements from the non-profit and for-profit sectors. They act a combination of elements of the non-profit and business sectors, creating something inherently different to both "a mixture of social and private faces" (Hayllar and Wettenhall, 2013: 207).

In this chapter for following definition will be used:

Social enterprises are organisations that trade to tackle social problems, improve communities, people's life chances, or the environment. They make their money from selling goods and services in the open market but they reinvest their profits back into the organisation or the local community (Social Enterprise UK, 2014).

This definition captures the values of commerce, empowerment and community ownership. In addition it is open enough to cover, not only 'pure' social enterprises, but also organisations that engage in social enterprise activities. The definition also captures the importance to social enterprise of social values, both in the activity it undertakes and in how it uses its profits.

The Purpose of Branding

De Chernatony and Dall'Olmo Riley (1998), following their review of definitions found in the literature, defined a brand as: "a complex multidimensional construct whereby managers augment products and services with values and this facilitates the process by which consumers confidently recognise and appreciate these values" (1998: 417).

Over time, the focus of branding has shifted. De Chernatony and Dall'Olmo Riley (1998) identified "A shift in emphasis from the notion of brands as logos to a more integrated view as the matching of a firm's emotional values with the performance and psychological values sought by the consumer" (1998: 418).

Brands serve a wide number of important functions:

- Brands create and maintain a point of difference between products and companies in a competitive environment (Hankinson 2001, Malik and Naeem 2012);
- Brands engender loyalty in customers (Haigh and Gilbert 2005);
- Brands simplify the recognition and selection process for customers (Biel 1992, Haigh and Gilbert 2005, Keller and Lehmann 2006, Kylander and Stone 2012);
- Brands are aspirational – attracting customers to products that reflect how they would like to be seen (Haigh and Gilbert 2005);
- Brands enable people to express themselves and project their own self-image (Haigh and Gilbert 2005, and Stride and Lee 2007);
- Brands communicate values (De Chernatony and Dall'Olmo Riley 1997).

Branding is important because it is an effective marketing tool that adds to the success of a business. Haigh and Gilbert (2005) describe it as a critical success factor for many organisations and it is considered an important means for creating and sustaining competitive advantage (Bouhlel *et al.* 2011).

Brands in Context

Brands have long been an essential component of marketing in for-profit organisations. However, until quite recently it was less commonplace in the non-profit sector, frequently perceived as being 'too commercial'. In research undertaken by Stride and Lee (2007) a senior communications director reported that the term brand had been regarded as a "dirty word" that would "commercialise and undermine the integrity of the mission" (2007: 112-113).

Until quite recently in so far as brands were used by non-profit organisations, it was primarily as a fundraising and communications tool. However, a growing number of them are now developing a more strategic approach, managing their brands to maximize social impact and to encourage tighter organisational cohesion (Kylander and Stone, 2012). Increasingly a strong brand is seen as critical to helping a non-profit to build operational capacity, galvanise support and maintain focus on the social mission (Kylander and Stone, 2012).

As commercial entities social enterprises embrace business processes and adopt the profit motive in order to support social benefits. That focus dictates a market oriented approach which includes marketing and, as an essential part of that, branding (Pitta and Kucher 2009). Thus, it is reasonable to assume that social enterprises do not share the same antipathy towards branding as non-profit organisations. It is more likely that they would pursue branding for the commercial advantages it undoubtedly provides.

Brand Personality

It is now accepted that brands are considered to have a personality (Aaker, 1999; Freling and Forbes, 2005; Sung and Tinkham, 2005). This is due to a natural human tendency called anthropomorphism which is the attribution of human characteristics to non-human things (Freling and Forbes, 2005). It has also been concluded that consumers have no difficulty in identifying personality traits in brands (Azouley and

Kapferer, 2003; Bouhlel *et al.* 2011) and that brand personality is not only attributed to tangible products but also to services (Freling and Forbes, 2005). Ferrandi *et al.* (2003) defined brand personality as "the set of human personality traits associated with a brand" (2003: 545).

Brand personality is an effective marketing tool which affects the relationship between consumers and the product or service in a number of ways. It can differentiate, and create competitive advantage in the consumer's minds, for brands that are otherwise indistinguishable from their competitors (Biel, 1992, Aaker, 1999; Freling and Forbes, 2005; Bouhlel *et al.*, 2011). It contributes to brand equity (Biel, 1992; Aaker, 1999; Bouhlel *et al.* 2011; Freling and Forbes, 2005) and provides a sustainable competitive advantage for a company (Das *et al.*, 2012). Brand personality is durable and therefore, if a positive image is formed in the minds of consumers, it can provide a significant asset for a company (Biel, 1992; Aaker, 1997). A well established brand personality can engender loyalty and strong emotional ties (Biel, 1992; Freling and Forbes, 2005).

Bouhlel *et al.* (2011) demonstrated that brand personality makes brands more desirable to the consumer. Consumers prefer brands that have strong, favourable personalities (Freling and Forbes, 2005) and ones associated with personality traits that are congruent with their own (Aaker, 1999; Bouhlel *et al.*, 2011). A brand's personality can project the brand's values (Freling and Forbes, 2005). This is of particular significance for non-profit organisations and social enterprises because they are defined as value driven organisations (Hankinson, 2001; Stride and Lee, 2007).

There is a clear consensus that individuals can differentiate between non-profit organisations on the basis of personality traits (Venable et al., 2005; Sargeant et al., 2008). At a sectorial level, Sargeant et al (2008) found that, distinct from the for-profit sector, personality traits are shared by the non-profit/charity sector as a whole. For example, they found that donors associate a particular set of personality traits with charities as a whole and assume the presence of these traits unless otherwise explicitly indicated. This has profound implications for non-profit brand management and points to that the importance of non-profit organisations emphasising their charitable status and thus creating a positive brand personality in the minds of consumers. Venable et al (2005) focused on the role that brands play in attracting support and donations and concluded that non-profit brand personality may influence potential donor's likelihood to contribute. Voeth and Herbst (2008: 77) contended that "contrary to for-profit brands, brand management in the non-profit sector should emphasise the central values of both the organisation and its supporters". According to Stride (2006) brand personality is one of the most effective tools that non-profit organisations can use to create identities that are based on core values and mission statements.

While there is a paucity of literature relating to brand personality in social enterprises, it is possible to draw on the literature that evidences the commercial value of brand personality in the for-profit sector and the important role brand personality plays in communicating values and attracting donations in the non-profit sector. It may be reasonably construed that, as a hybrid of those two sectors, social enterprises could benefit from the positive impacts brand personality brings to both camps.

This chapter proposes three hypotheses:
- Firstly, the 'charitable/social' element of social enterprises, if well communicated through an appropriate brand personality, will have a positive impact on the attractiveness of its products to consumers;
- Secondly, the central role of values in social enterprise makes brand personality a particularly useful marketing tool;
- Thirdly, as social enterprises aim to be commercially successful, brand personality provides an ideal mechanism to assist in this process.

Measuring Brand Personality

A strong brand personality is invaluable in building brand equity. As a consequence, reliable, valid and practical measurement tools are essential (Geuens *et al*,. 2009). A reliable and accurate brand personality scale would:
- Help managers to segment their markets and know their customers better (Das *et al.*, 2012);
- Help them to understand how their customers perceive their brand and that of their competitors (Das *et al.*, 2012);
- Enable managers to monitor changes in brand personality over time, particularly in situations when an attempt is being made to change an existing brand personality (Das *et al.*, 2012);

- Enable researchers and marketing managers to identify benchmark personality brands and to compare personalities of brands across product categories (Aaker, 1997).

The development of many brand personality measurement instruments is grounded in the concept of personality in psychology. In identifying and measuring human personality traits, the theory of what's known as the 'Big Five' is widely accepted. Adjectives or 'markers' are attributed to each of the 'Big Five' human personality dimensions (Saucier, 1994; Goldberg, 1992) and can be used by psychologists to form a quick evaluation of an individual's personality.

The five human personality dimensions, often labelled OCEAN, are:
- **O**penness to new experiences;
- **C**onscientiousness including traits such as scrupulousness and trustworthiness;
- **E**xtraversion including traits such as openness to others, sociability and impulsivity;
- **A**greeableness including traits such as kindness, modesty, trust and altruism;
- **N**euroticism including traits such as anxiety, instability and nervousness.

The first comprehensive and robust brand personality instrument was developed by Jennifer Aaker (1997). In her work she drew on research on the 'Big Five' human personality structure to develop a theoretical framework of brand personality dimensions. She identified five brand personality dimensions- sincerity, excitement, competence, sophistication and ruggedness.

Brand Personality Instruments and the Non-profit Sector
Venable et al. (2005) sought to refine and develop existing brand personality measurement for non-profit organisations. They found that Aaker's (1997) five brand personality traits could also be applied to describe non-profit organisations. However, they identified two specific and important findings in relation to non-profits: their social importance as kind, caring and compassionate and their perceived trustworthiness (Venable et al., 2005). Thus they adjusted Aaker's scale

so that it was more applicable to the non-profit sector. This new scale was a four factor instrument in which the brand personality dimensions were integrity, sophistication, ruggedness and nurturance.

Voeth and Herbst also undertook research which explicitly aimed 'to present a brand personality scale that is directed towards the distinct characteristics of the non-profit sector" (2008: 73). They used Aaker (1997) as a starting point but acknowledged that 'it is not advisable to transfer the 'brand personality scale' to the non-profit sector without adaptation.' They concluded that "the structure of brand personality in the non-profit sector differs significantly from the structure of consumer brands" (2008: 93). The scale developed by Voeth and Herbst (2008) had three dimensions: social competence and trust, emotion and assertiveness and sophistication.

These, and other studies used Aaker's scale as a starting point. However, this scale was developed in the for-profit sector and it is important to question the potential impact this might have on the instrument's validity for use within the non-profit sector.

Brand personality measurement instruments in a social enterprise context

While researchers have recognised the importance of developing brand personality instruments in and for the non-profit sector in recognition of its difference to the for-profit sector, no brand personality measurement instrument has been developed specifically for social enterprises. As social enterprises are inherently different to both for-profit and non-profit organisations they too merit the development of their own distinct brand personality measurement instrument.

As can be seen from above, attempts by researchers to employ or validate brand personality instruments (for example in a different cultural context) has frequently resulted in the original framework being amended with the addition or deletion of personality dimensions (Aaker *et al.* 2001, Ambroise *et al.* 2005, Venable *et al.* 2005, Sung and Tinkham 2005, Smith *et al.* 2006). This suggests that attempts to apply existing brand personality measurement instrument to social enterprises could result in the development of a new scale which would be appropriate to the character of social enterprise.

The mixed quantitative and qualitative approach advocated by Arora and Stoner (2009) proposed a two stage process; firstly, the use of a quantitative instrument such as Aaker's scale (1997) followed up with a qualitative research dimension. This approach could suggest that application of an instrument which is broadly compatible could result in its adaptation so that it is applicable in a social enterprise context. It is likely that because social enterprises are so distinct from for-profit and nonprofit organisations that distinct brand personality dimensions would emerge from the use of an existing brand personality instrument and a new social enterprise viable instrument would be created.

Conclusion

This chapter has proposed three hypotheses:

The 'charitable/social' element of social enterprises, if sufficiently expressed through an appropriate brand personality, will have a positive impact on the attractiveness of their products to consumers.

Research undertaken by Bennett and Gabriel (2000) on charities that trade, suggests that brand personality could have a positive impact on the sale of products in a social enterprise context. The study aimed to identify the impact of charity brand identity on the likelihood of existing customers responding favourably to the introduction of new and unrelated products. The study concluded that having positive brand personalities for charity products enabled the charity to introduce new products with high levels of success.

It seems reasonable to draw the conclusion that social enterprises could benefit from employing marketing strategies that capitalize on their charity like brand personality traits to provide them with competitive advantage.

The central role of values in social enterprises makes brand personality a particularly useful marketing tool.

The main difference between social enterprises and for-profit organisations is that social enterprises are 'value driven' or 'value based' and for-profit organisations are not (Dart 2004, Hallyar and Wettenhall 2013). A brand's personality can project the brand's values (Freling and Forbes 2005). According to De Chernatory and Dell'Olmo Riley (1998) strong and successful brands show a greater degree of congruence between the values firms develop for them and the rational and emotional needs of their customers. Brand personality is particularly effective at communicating values and people form close attachments to brands with which they share values (Freling and Forbes 2005). As social enterprises are highly value driven it could be concluded that brand personality is a potentially powerful marketing tool for social enterprises.

Brand personality is an effective way of increasing the success of a business. As social enterprises aim to be commercially successful, brand personality provides an ideal mechanism to assist in this process.

'Simply put, brand personality really does make a difference' (Freling and Forbes 2005: 160). 'Several comparisons and studies point to the fact that brands with strong personalities outperform brands without' (Heding *et al.* 2008: 118). As commercial entities social enterprises embrace business processes. Unlike in the case of non-profits, there is no conflict between their social purpose and their benefitting from 'commercial' activities such as marketing as they are, at heart commercial ventures themselves.

There is a need for significantly more research into brand personality and brand personality measurement in the context of social enterprise. There is little to be found in the current literature. However, from what can be inferred from the literature relating to non-profit organisations (which is itself scant) with which social enterprise shares many characteristics, brand personality could provide a rich vein for future research.

REFERENCES

A

Aaker, J. 1997. "Dimensions of Brand Personality." *Journal of Marketing Research*, Volume XXXIV: 347-356.

Aaker, J. 1999. "The Malleable Self: The Role of Self-expression in Persuasion." *Journal of Marketing Research*, Volume XXXVI: 45-57

Aikins, K. 2009. *The Ireland Funds Philanthropy and Fundraising Toolkit.* Dublin: Impress Printing Works.

Akkermans, H. 2001. "Renga: A systems approach to facilitating inter-organizational network development." *System Dynamics Review*, Volume 17(3): 179-193.

Alter, K. 2007. *Social Enterprise Typology.* [Online] Available from: http://www.virtueventures.com/setypology.pdf [Accessed 27/10/14].

Ambroise, L, Ferrandi, J, Merunka, D, Valette-Florence, P. 2005. "Development Of A Brand Personality Scale And Application To Two Supermarket Brands", Institut d'Administration des Entreprises, Clos Guiot, 13540 Puyricard, France.

Amin, A. 2002. "Ethnicity and the Multicultural City." *Environment and Planning A*, Volume 34(6): 959-980.

Amin, A., Cameron, A., and Hudson, R. 2003. *Placing the social economy.* London: Routledge.

Amin, A. 2009. "Locating the Social Economy." In *The Social Economy – International Perspectives on Economic Solidarity*, ed. A. Amin. London: Zed Books.

Arora, R, Stoner, C. 2009. "A mixed method approach to understanding brand personality." *Journal of Product & Brand Management*, Volume 18(4): 272 – 283.

Austin, J. Stevenson, H. and Wei-Skillern, J. 2006. "Social and Commercial Entrepreneurship: Same, Different, or Both?" *Entrepreneurship Theory and Practice*, Volume 30(1): 1-22.

B

Baines, P., Fill, C. and Page, K. 2011. *Marketing.* (2nd, Ed.) Oxford: Oxford University Press.

Bell, J. Masoka, J. and Zimmerman, S. 2010. *Nonprofit Sustainability: Making Strategic Decisions for Financial Viability.* San Francisco: Jossey-Bass.

Bénabou, R. and Tirole, J. 2002. "Self-Confidence and Personal Motivation." *Quarterly Journal of Economics*, Volume 117(3): 871-915.

Bennett R, Gabriel, H, (2000) "Charity Affiliation As A Determinant Of Product Purchase Decisions." *Journal of Product and Brand Management*, Volume 9(4): 255-270.

Bergenholtz, C., and Waldstrom, C. 2011. "Inter-Organizational Network Studies—A Literature Review". *Industry and Innovation*, Volume 18(6): 539-562.

Biel, A L. 1992. "How Brand Image Drives Brand Equity." *Journal of Advertising Research*, Volume 32 (6): 6-12.

Birdthistle, N. and Fleming, P. 2007. "Under the microscope: a profile of the family business in Ireland." *The Irish Journal of Management: Special Edition on Entrepreneurship*, Volume 28(2): 133-168.

Borzaga, C., and Santuari, A. (Eds.). 1998. *Social Enterprises and New Employment in Europe*. Regione Autonoma Trentino-Alto Adige: Cooperation Department.

Boschee. J., Nitze. L and Gray. C. 2010 *Social enterprise: A powerful engine for economic and social development*. [Online] Available from: http://community-wealth.org/content/social-enterprise-powerful-engine-economic-and-social-development [Accessed 27/10/14].

Bouhlel, O, Mzoughi, N, Hadiji, D, Slimane, I. 2011. "Brand Personality's Influence on the Purchase Intention: A Mobile Marketing Case." *International Journal of Business and Management*, Volume 6(9): 210-227.

Broad, G. and Saunders, M. 2008. *Social enterprises and the Ontario disability support program: A policy perspective on employing persons with disabilities*. Centre for the Study of Co-operatives, University of Saskatchewan.

Bowman, W. 2011. "Financial Capacity and Sustainability of Ordinary Non-profits." *Non-profit Management and Leadership*, Volume 22(1): 37–51.

Burge, P., Ouellette-Kuntz, H., and Lysaght, R. 2007. "Public views on employment of people with intellectual disabilities." *Journal of Vocational Rehabilitation*, Volume 26(1): 29-37.

C

Care Farming 2014. *What is Care Farming* [Online] Available from: http://www.carefarminguk.org/ [Accessed 06/05/2014].

Care Farming West Midlands 2014. *Willowdene Farm* [Online] Available from: http://carefarmingwm.org.uk/care_farm/willowdene-farm/ [Accessed 06/05/14].

Carlsson, S. A. 2003. "Knowledge Managing and Knowledge Management Systems in Inter-organizational Networks." *Knowledge and Process Management,* Volume 10(3): 194-206.

Chiu, C., Hsu, M., and Wang, E. 2006. "Understanding knowledge sharing in virtual communities: An integration of social capital and social cognitive theories." *Decision Support Systems,* Volume 42(3): 1872-1888.

Clann Credo. 2010. *Adding Value, Delivering Change, The Role of Social Enterprise in National Recovery,* [Online] Available from: http://www.clanncredo.ie/gfx/uploads/textbox/SETFBrochureSml_07_0 6.pdf [Accessed 27/10/14].

Clann Credo. 2011. *From the Ground Up. How Social Finance can help Communities Regenerate and Create Jobs,* Dublin: Clann Credo.

Clarke, A., and Eustace, A. 2009. *Exploring Social In Nine Areas In Ireland.* Dublin: Eustace Patterson Limited.

Cluid Housing Association. 2014. *Annual Report 2013.* Dublin: Cluid Housing Association.

Cohen, J. 1995. *Associations and Democracy.* London: Verso.

Community Workers Cooperative. 2014. *CWC Alignment Update #3 July 2014.* [Online] Available from: http://www.cwc.ie/wp-content/uploads/2014/07/CWC-Alignment-3-July-2014.pdf [Accessed 27/10/14].

CSO. 2005. *Survey of Family Businesses in Ireland, Services Sector 2005.* [Online] Available from: http://www.cso.ie/en/media/csoie/releasespublications/documents/serv ices/2005/fbi2005.pdf [Accessed 27/10/14].

CSO. 2012. *Profile 8: Our Bill of Health.* Dublin: Government Publications Office.

Curtis, A. 2010. "Community Services Programme: is it the most suitable government funded programme to support community groups." Masters thesis. University College Cork.

D

Dart, R. 2004. "The Legitimacy of Social Enterprise." *Nonprofit Management & Leadership,* Volume 14(4): 411 - 424.

Das, G., Guin, K. and Datta, B. 2012. "Developing Brand Personality Scales: a literature Review." *IUP Journal of Brand Management*, Volume 9(2): 44-63.

De Chernatory, L. and Dall'Olmo Rily, F. 1998. "Defining a brand: beyond the Literature with Experts' Interpretations." *Journal of Marketing Management*, Volume 14(4): 417-433.

DECLG. 2011. *Housing Policy Statement*. Dublin: Government Publications Office.

Donaldson, B., and O'Toole, T. 2002. *Strategic Market Relationships: From Strategy to Implementation*. Chichester: John Wiley and Sons.

Doyle, G. 2010. *Social Enterprise – An Untapped Resource*. [Online) Available from: http://www.workingnotes.ie/index.php/item/social-enterprise-an-untapped-resource [Accessed 27/10/14].

Doyle, G. and Lalor, T. (eds.) 2012. *Social Enterprise in Ireland - A People's Economy*. Cork: Oak Tree Press.

Durham University School of Applied Social Services 2011. *Can social enterprises reduce reoffending?* [Online] Available from: https://www.dur.ac.uk/resources/sass/research/briefings/ResearchBriefing4 [Accessed 02/03/14].

E

EMES. 2014. *Social Enterprise*. [Online] Available from: http://www.emes.net/about-us/focus-areas/social-enterprise [Accessed 15/07/2014].

ENHR. 2013. *The European Network of Social Housing* [Online] Available from: http://www.enhr.net/socialhousing.php [Accessed 27/10/14].

Enterprise Ireland. 2005. *Transforming Irish Industry: Enterprise Ireland Strategy 2005-2007*. Dublin: Enterprise Ireland.

European Commission. 1994. *Structural Funds Grant – Million to Industrial Development in Ireland*. [Online] Available from: http://europa.eu/rapid/press-release_IP-94-1058_en.htm [Accessed 27/10/14].

European Commission. 2011. *Social Business Initiative - Creating a favourable climate for social enterprises, key stakeholders in the social economy and innovation*. [Online] Available from: http://eur-lex.europa.eu/LexUriServ/LexUriServ.do?uri=COM:2011:0682:FIN:EN:PDF [Accessed 27/10/14].

F

Ferrandi, J.M., Merunka D., Valette-Florence P. and De Barnier V. 2003. "The Transfer of a Reduced Human Personality Scale to Brands: An Initial Cross-Cultural Test." *International Research Seminar on Marketing Communications and Consumer Behavior*, La Londe les Maures, Volume 5: 545-561.

Fine, B. 2007. "Financialisation, Poverty, and Marxist Political Economy", Poverty and Capital Conference, 2-4 July 2007, University of Manchester [Online] Available from https://eprints.soas.ac.uk/5685/1/brooks.pdf [Accessed 27/10/14].

Fine, B. 2013. "Beyond the Developmental State". In *Beyond the Developmental State – Industrial Policy in the Twenty-First Century*, ed. B. Fine, J. Saraswati, J. and D. Tavaschi. London: Pluto Press.

Flora, C.B. 2006. "Are entrepreneurs born or made?" *Rural Development News*, Volume 28(4): 1-7.

Forestry Commission. 2014. *Forest Research – Using Nature in Offender Rehabilitation* [Online] Available from: http://www.forestry.gov.uk/website/forestresearch.nsf/ByUnique/INFD -6ZABBK [Accessed 13/07/2014].

Forfás. 2007. Ireland's Co-operative Sector. Online] Available from: http://www.forfas.ie/media/cooperative_sector_2007.pdf Accessed 27/10/2014].

Forfás. 2013. *Social Enterprise in Ireland: Sectoral Opportunities and Policy Issues.* [Online] Available from: http://www.forfas.ie/publication/search.jsp?ft=/publications/2013/title,1 1029,en.php [Accessed 16/7/2014].

Freling, T. and Forbes, L. 2005. "An examination of brand personality through methodological triangulation." *Brand Management*, Volume 13(2): 148 – 162.

G

Gartner, W.B. 1990. "What Are We Talking About When We Talk About Entrepreneurship?" *Journal of Business Venturing*, Volume 5(1): 15-28.

Geuens, M. and De Wulf Weijters, K. 2009. "A new measure of brand personality." *International Journal of Research in Marketing*, Volume 26: 97- 107.

Goldberg, L. 1992. "The Development of Markers for the Big Five Factor Structure." *Psychological Assessment*, Volume 4(1): 26-42.

Grayling, C. 2012. *Prison gates mentor plan for released inmates* [Online] Available from: http://www.bbc.co.uk/news/uk-20399401 [Accessed 15/05/2014].

Grierson, J. 2013. *Reoffending rate increases* [Online] Available from: http://www.independent.co.uk/news/uk/crime/reoffending-rate-increases-8475391.html [Accessed 03/06/2014].

Growing Well. 2014. *Growing Well Annual Report* [Online] Available from: http://www.growingwell.co.uk/about-us.aspx [Accessed 02/06/14].

H

Hackler, D. and Saxton, G.D. 2007. "The strategic use of information technology by non-profit organizations: Increasing capacity and untapped potential." *Public Administration Review*, Volume 67(3): 474-487.

Haigh, D. and Gilbert, S. 2005. "Valuing not-for-profit and charity brands – real insight or just smoke and mirrors." *International Journal of Nonprofit and Voluntary Sector Marketing*, Volume 10(2): 107 – 119.

Hankinson, P. 2001. "Brand Orientation in the Charity Sector: A Framework for Discussion and Research." *International Journal of Nonprofit and Voluntary Sector Marketing*, Volume 6(3): 231 – 242.

Hay, C. and Wincott, D. 2012. *The Political Economy of European Welfare Capitalism*. Basingstoke: Palgrave Macmillan.

Hayllar, M. and Wettenhall, R. 2013. "As Public Goes Private, Social Emerges: The Rise of Social Enterprise." *Public Organization Review*, Volume 13(2): 207 – 217.

Heckman, J. 2013. *Giving Kids a Fair Chance*. Massachusetts: Boston Review Books.

Heding, T., Knudtzen, C. and Mugens, B. 2008. *Brand Management - Research, theory and practice*. London: Routledge.

Hickie, A. 1995. "Handing over the family business." *The Sunday Business Post*, 9 April, page 18.

Higgins, M.D. 2011. The *President of Michael D. Higgins – Inaugural Address* [Online]. Available from http://www.president.ie/work-in-ireland/ [Accessed 27/10/14].

Hine, R., Peacock, J. and Pretty, J. 2008. *Care farming in the UK: Evidence and Opportunities* [Online]. Available from: http://www.carefarminguk.org/sites/carefarminguk.org/files/Care%20F

arming%20in%20the%20UK%20-%20Essex%20Uni%20Report.pdf
[Accessed 10/06/2014].

Hurley, S. 2012. *Helping or hindering heroes? UK Armed Forces Veterans Literature Review*. London: Ministry of Defence.

Hutt, M. D., and Speh, T. W. 2007. *Business Marketing Management: B2B* (9th Ed.). Mason, Ohio: Thomson South-Western.

Hynes, B. 2009. "Growing the Social Enterprise – Issues and Challenges." *Social Enterprise Journal*, Volume 5(2): 114-125.

I

IASE 2014. *Irish Association of Supported Employment (IASE) Strategic Plan 2014 – 2016*. [Online] Available from: www.iase.ie/documents/IASEStrategy2014-2016.pdf [Accessed 27/10/14].

ISEN 2013. *About Us*. [Online], Available from: http://www.socent.ie/about-us/ [Accessed 17/02/2014].

J

Jayawarna, D. 2010. *Social Enterprise Bootstrapping as a Strategic Response to Recession*. [Online] Available from: www.isbe.org.uk/content/assets/Liverpool_University.pdf [Accessed 27/10/14].

K

Katz, E. and Kauder, R. 2011. *Social Enterprise Businesses: A Strategy for Creating Good Jobs for People with Disabilities*. West Orange: John J. Heldrich Center for Workforce Development and the Kessler Foundation (joint publication).

Katz, R.A. and Page, A. 2010. "Role of Social Enterprise." *Vermont Law Review*, Volume 35: 59-103.

Keller, K, Lehmann, D, (2006) "Brands and Branding: Research Findings and Future Priorities." *Marketing Science*, Volume 25(6): 740–759.

Kirsh, B., Stergiou-Kita, M., Gewurtz, R., Dawson, D., Krupa, T., Lysaght, R., and Shaw, L. 2009. "From margins to mainstream: What do we know about work integration for persons with brain injury, mental illness and intellectual disability?" *Work*, Volume 32(4): 391-405.

Kylander, N. and Stone, C. 2012. "The Role of the Brand in the non-profit Sector." *Stanford Social Innovation Review*, Volume 35(1): 37-41.

L

Lackéus, M. 2013. *Developing Entrepreneurial Competencies: an Action Based Approach and Classification in Education* (Unpublished licentiate thesis) Chalmers University, Gothenburg, Sweden.

Leon, P. 2001. *Four Pillars of Financial Sustainability - Resources for Success Series (Volume 2).* Arlington: US Aid for International Development.

Low, C. 2006. "A framework for the governance of social enterprise". *International Journal of Social Economics*, Volume 33(5): 376-385.

Lysaght, R. 2010. "Editorial: Employment as a Path to Inclusion." *Journal of Policy and Practice in Intellectual Disabilities*, Volume 7(4): 233-234.

M

Major, G., and Boby, M. 2000. *Equity Devaluation, The Rarity of Democratic Firms, and "Profit Shares".* [Online] Available from: www.democraticbusiness.co.uk/vanekps.html [Accessed 23/3/2013].

Malik, M.E., Naeem, B. 2012. "Aaker's Brand Personality Framework: A Critical Commentary." *Journal of Basic and Applied Scientific Research*, Volume 2(12): 11992-11996.

Marques, J. 2014. *Social and Solidarity Economy - Between Emancipation and Reproduction.* [Online] Available from: http://www.unrisd.org/marques [Accessed 27/10/2014].

McClelland, D.C. 1976. *The Achievement Motive.* New York: Irvington Publishers

Melhuish, E. 2004. *A Literature Review of the Impact of Early Years Provision on Young Children.* London: National Audit Office.

Mentzas, G., Apostolou, D., Kafentzis, K., and Georgolios, P. 2006. "Inter-organizational networks for knowledge sharing and trading." *Information Technology Management*, Volume 7: 259-276.

Merrett, C.D. and Walzer, D. 2004. *Cooperatives and Local Development – Theory and Applications for the 21st Century.* London: M.E. Sharpe.

Ministry of Defence. 2014. *The Mercian Regiment* [Online] Available from: http://www.army.mod.uk/infantry/regiments/23998.aspx#25978 [Accessed. 19/07/2014].

Ministry of Justice. 2014. *Transforming rehabilitation* [Online] Available from: http://www.justice.gov.uk/transforming-rehabilitation [Accessed 19/7/2014]

Mu, J. Peng, G. and Love, E. 2008. "Interfirm Network, Social Capital, and Knowledge Flow." *Journal of Knowledge Management*, Volume 12(4), 86-100.

Myers, M.D. 2008. *Qualitative Research in Business and Management.* London: SAGE Publications.

N

NACRO 2010. *A guide to working with veterans in custody* [Online] Available from:
https://www.nacro.org.uk/data/files/working-with-veterans-810.pdf [Accessed 27/10/14].

Nahapiet, J. and Ghoshai, S. 1998. "Social Capital, Intellectual Capital, and Organizational Advantage." *Academy of Management Review*, Volume 23(2): 242-266.

NDA. 2010. *Developing Services for People with Disabilities: A synthesis paper summarising the key learning of experiences in selected jurisdictions.* Dublin: National Disability Authority.

NESC. 2014. *Social Housing at the Crossroads: Possibilities for Investment, Provision and Cost Rental.* Dublin: National Economic and Social Development Office.

NEF. 2014. *Creating a Theory of Change* [Online] Available from:
http://www.nef-consulting.co.uk/our-services/training-capacity-building/masterclasses/creating-a-theory-of-change/ [Accessed 03/07/14].

Noel, N. M., and Luckett, M. 2014. "The benefits, satisfaction, and perceived value of small business membership in a chamber of commerce." *International Journal of Nonprofit and Voluntary Sector Marketing*, Volume 19(1): 27-39.

Noya, A. 2009. *The Changing Boundaries of Social Enterprise.* [Online] Available from: http://www.fcssbc.ca/sf-docs/socent/oecd-social-enterprise.pdf [Accessed 27/10/14].

O

Ó Broin, D. 2009. "Institutionalising Social Partnership in Ireland." In *Power, Dissent and democracy – Civil Society and the State in Ireland,* eds. D. Ó Broin and P. Kirby. Dublin: A&A Farmar.

Ó Broin, D. and Kirby, P. 2009. "Creating a parallel state: the development of Irish civil society in the late 19th and early 20th centuries." In *Power, Dissent and democracy – Civil Society and the State in*

Ireland, eds. D. Ó Broin and P. Kirby. Dublin: A&A Farmar.

Ó Broin, D. 2012. "Social enterprise or social entrepreneurship: economic solidarity or market hegemony?" In *Social Enterprise in Ireland: A People's Economy?* eds. G. Doyle and T. Lalor. Cork: Oak Tree Press

OECD. 1999. *Social Enterprises*. Paris: OECD.

OECD. 2007. *The Social Economy - Building Inclusive Economies*. Paris: OECD.

OECD. 2010. *Entrepreneurship, SMEs and Innovation*. Paris: OECD.

OECD. 2012. *A Quality Toolbox for Early Childhood Education and Care*. Paris: OECD.

OECD. 2013. *Policy Brief on Social Entrepreneurship - Entrepreneurial Activities in Europe*. Paris: OECD.

O'Neill, G. 2014. *Restoration of trust key to halting 50pc slide in donations to charitable causes*. Irish Independent, March 3, page 9.

Ó Riain, S. 2014. *The Rise and Fall of the Celtic Tiger*. Cambridge: Cambridge University Press.

Ostrom, E. 1999. "Crossing the great divide. Co-production, synergy & development, polycentric governance and development." In *Reading from the workshop in political theory and policy analysis* ed. M.D. McGinnes. Ann Arbor: University of Michigan Press.

P

Palma, G. 2009. "The Revenge of the Market on the Rentiers: Why Neo-Liberal Reports of the End of History Turned out to Be Premature." *Cambridge Journal of Economics*, Volume 33(4): 829–869.

Parmenter, T.R. 2011. *Promoting Training and Employment Opportunities for People with Intellectual Disabilities, International Experience*. Geneva: ILO.

Pearce, J. 2003. *Social Enterprise in Anytown*. London: Calouste Gulbenkian Foundation.

Pearse, J. 2005. *The Future of Social Enterprise in the UK*. [Online], Available from: www.caledonia.org.uk/papers/Future-of-UK-Social-Enterprises.doc [Accessed 5/7/2014].

Pestoff, V. 2012. "Co-production and Third Sector Social Services in Europe: Some Concepts and Evidence." *VOLUNTAS*, Volume 23(4): 1102-1118.

Pitta, D.A. and Kucher, J.H. 2009. "Social enterprises as consumer products: the case of vehicles for change." *Journal of Product & Brand Management,* Volume 18(2): 154-158.

Price Waterhouse Coopers. 2012. 'Family Business Survey 2012: Findings for Ireland. [Online] Available from: http://download.pwc.com/ie/pubs/2012_family_business_survey_findi ngs_for_ireland.pdf [Accessed 27/10/14].

Prince, M. J. 2014. "Locating a Window of Opportunity in the Social Economy: Canadians with Disabilities and Labour Market Challenges." *Canadian Journal of Nonprofit and Social Economy Research,* Volume 5(1): 6-20.

Putnam, R. D. 1995. "Bowling Alone: America's declining social capital." *Journal of Democracy,* Volume 6(1): 65-68.

Q

Qureshi, S. S. 1995. "Organisations and Networks: Theoretical Considerations and a Case Study of Networking across Organisations". PhD Dissertation. University of London.

R

Robbins, P. 2013. *Understanding Innovation: Contemporary Issues in Innovation Management.* Harlow: Pearson.

Rosen, M.J. 2005. "Doing well by doing right: A fundraisers guide to ethical decision-making." *International Journal of Nonprofit and Voluntary Sector Marketing,* Volume 10: 175-181.

Rotter, J.B. 1954. *Social Learning and Clinical Psychology.* New York: Prentice Hall.

Russel, L., and Scott, D. 2007. *Social Enterprise in Practice: Developmental Stories from the Voluntary and Community Sector.* West Malling: Charities Aid Foundation.

S

Sargeant, A., Hudson, J. and West, D. 2008. "Conceptualising brand values in the charity sector: the relationship between sector, cause and organisation." *The Service Industries Journal,* Volume 28(5): 615 – 632.

Saucier, G. 1994. "Mini-Markers: A Brief Version of Goldberg's Unipolar Big 5 Markers." *Journal of Personality Assessment,* Volume 63(3): 506-516.

Sayer, A. 2000. "Equality and Moral Economy." Presented at the

Equality Studies Centre 10th Anniversary Conference, University college Dublin, December 15th 2000. [Online] Available from: http://www.lancs.ac.uk/fass/sociology/papers/sayer-equality-and-moral-economy.pdf [Accessed 27/10/2014].

SEETF. 2010. *Adding Value - Delivering Change: The Role of Social Enterprise in National Recovery*. Dublin: Social Enterprise and Entrepreneurship Task Force

SEETF. 2012. *Unlocking the Potential of Social Enterprise and Entrepreneurship*, Dublin: Social Enterprise and Entrepreneurship Task Force.

Shahmash, S. 2010. *Social Enterprises: Creating Jobs and Community Wellness One Small Business at a Time*. Vancouver: ISIS Research Centre, University of British Columbia.

Sheehy, J. 2006. *Family Business Succession Planning*. [Online] Available from: www.bdo.ie/files/pdf/pubs/fbs/bdo-family-business-v3-web.pdf [Accessed 27/10/14].

Shefsky, L. E. 1994. *Entrepreneurs are Made not Born*. New York: McGraw-Hill.

Shier, M., Graham, J. R. and Jones, M. E. 2009. "Barriers to employment as experienced by disabled people: a qualitative analysis in Calgary and Regina, Canada." *Disability and Society*, Volume 24(1): 63-75.

Smiddy, A. 2002. *Welcome and Introduction*. 6 March, National Family Business Seminar, Plato Ireland, Dublin.

Smith, A.C.T., Graetz, B.R. and Westerbeek, H.M. 2006. "Brand personality in a membership-based organisation." *International Journal of Nonprofit Voluntary Sector Marketing*, Volume 11(3): 251–266.

Social Enterprise Alliance. 2014. *The Case for Social Enterprise Alliance*. [Online] Available from: https://www.se-alliance.org/what-is-social-enterprise [Accessed 15/7/2014].

Social Enterprise UK. 2014. About Us. [Online] Available from: http://www.socialenterprise.org.uk/about/about-social-enterprise [Accessed 27/10/2014].

Social Exclusion Unit. 2002. *Reducing Re-offending* [Online] Available from: http://www.restorativejustice.org/articlesdb/articles/4219 [Accessed 02/06/2014].

Social Firms UK. 2009. *Proving the value of social firms/ impact measurement* [Online] Available from: www.socialfirmsuk.co.uk/about-social-forms/-value-socil-firms-and-proviing-it [Accessed 03/07/2014].

Social Impact Consulting. 2012. *Green Light: Creating Jobs through Social Enterprise.* [Online] Available from: http://www.wates.co.uk/sites/all/modules/filemanager/files/CR/Social_ Enterprise_in_the_Housing_Sector.pdf [Accessed 27/10/14].

Sontag-Padilla, L., Staplefoote, B.L. and Morganti, K.G. 2011. *Financial Sustainability for Nonprofit Organizations: A Review of the Literature.* Santa Monica: Rand Corporation.

Start Strong. 2013. *Shaping the Future,* Dublin: Start Strong.

Start Strong. 2014. *The double dividend: childcare that's affordable and high quality - Submission review of funding schemes for early care and education,* Dublin: Start Strong.

Strang France, E. 2007. *Applying social enterprise approaches to services for children, young people and families.* London: VCS Engage.

Stride, H.
2006. "An investigation into the values dimensions of branding: implications for the charity sector." *International Journal of Nonprofit & Voluntary Sector Marketing,* Volume 11(2): 115-124.

Stride, H, Lee, S. 2007. "No Logo? No way. Branding in the Non-Profit Sector." *Journal of Marketing Management,* Volume 23(1): 107 – 122.

Sung, Y. and Tinkham, S.F. 2005. "Brand Personality Structures in the United States and Korea: Common and Culture-Specific Factors." *Journal of Consumer Psychology,* Volume 15(4): 334-350.

T

The Code. 2014. *Voluntary Code of Practice for Social Enterprise in Scotland, The Criteria.* [Online], Available from: http://www.se-code.net/the-code-2/the-criteria/ [Accessed 15/7/2014].

The Howard League for Penal Reform. 2009. *Leaving Forces Life: The issue of transition* [Online] Available from: www.gov.uk/government/uploads/system/uploads/attachment_data/fil e/28111/ Leaving_Forces_Life.pdf [Accessed 19/07/2014].

The Howard League for Penal Reform. 2010. *Barbed what happened next? Follow up story of a prison social enterprise* [Online] Available from: http://www.howardleague.org/work/ [Accessed 19/07/2014].

The Howard League for Penal Reform. 2011. *Business Behind Bars* [Online] Available from: http://www.howardleague.org/work/ [Accessed 19/07/2014].

The Wheel. (2009). *Beyond Budget 2010: Imagining a new future.* [Online], Available from: from:

http://www.wheel.ie/sites/default/files/LC%20winter%2009.pdf [Accessed 14/5/2014].

The Wheel. 2014. *A Portrait of Ireland's Non Profit Sector 2014*. Dublin: The Wheel in partnership with Crowe Howarth

The World Café Community Foundation. (n.d.). *World Café Method*. [Online], Available from: http://www.theworldcafe.com/method.html [Accessed 23/5/2014].

Thomke, S. 2003. "R&D Comes to Services." *Harvard Business Review,* Volume 81(4): 70-79.

Thompson, A.A., Peteraf, M.A., Gamble, J.E., Stickland, A.J., Janes, A. and Sutton, C. 2013. *Crafting and Executing Strategy. The Quest for Competitive Advantage*. Berkshire: McGraw Hill.

Trembath, D., Balandin, S., Stancliffe, R. J. and Togher, L. 2010. "Employment and volunteering for adults with intellectual disability." *Journal of Policy and Practice in Intellectual Disabilities*, Volume 7(4): 235-238.

Tsai, W., and Ghoshai, S. 1998. "Social Capital and Value Creation: The role of intrafirm networks." *Academy of Management Journal,* Volume 41(4), 464-476.

U

UK Agriculture 2014. *Crisis in agriculture and British farming* [Online] Available from: http://www.ukagriculture.com/farming_today/farming_crisis.cfm [Accessed 13/07/2014].

Unger, R. 2009. *The Left Alternative*. London: Verso.

UNRISD. 2014. Social and Solidarity Economy and the Challenge of Sustainable Development. [Online] Available from: http://www.unrisd.org/ssetaskforce-positionpaper [Accessed 27/10/2014].

Utting, P. 2013. *Social and Solidarity Economy: A Pathway to Socially Sustainable Development?* [Online] Available from: http://www.unrisd.org/unrisd/website/newsview.nsf/%28httpNews%29/AB920B156339500AC1257B5C002C1E96?OpenDocument [Accessed 27/10/2014].

Utting, P., van Dijk, N. Mathei, M. 2014. *Social and Solidarity Economy - Is There a New Economy in the Making?* [Online] Available from: http://www.unrisd.org/utting-et-al [Accessed 27/10/2014].

V

Venable, B., Rose, G., Bush, V. and Gilbert, F. 2005. "The Role of Brand Personality in Charitable Giving: An Assessment and Validation", *Journal of the Academy of Marketing Science*, Volume 33(3): 295-312.

Veteransfarm. 2009. *About Veterans Farm*. [Online] Available from: http://veteransfarm.org/?page_id=10 [Accessed 13/07/2014]

Voeth, M. and Herbst, U. 2008. "The Concept of Brand Personality as an Instrument for Advanced Non-Profit Branding – An empirical Analysis." *Journal of Nonprofit & Public Sector Marketing*, Volume 19(1): 71-97.

Vujić, S. 2011. "Introducing SELUSI Conceptualization of a Social Enterprise and SELUSI Methodology of Gathering Data on Social Enterprises." Presented at Social Enterprise and Social Business Innovation in Europe: Final Project Conference, 6th and 7th October 2011. University of Bath.

W

Welsh Government 2014. *Welsh Government 'Community Grown Food Action Plan* [Online] Available from: http://wales.gov.uk/topics/environmentcountryside/foodandfisheries/foodandmarketdevelopmentpubs/comgrownfoodplan/?lang=en [Accessed 13/07/14].

Welsh Co-operative and Mutuals Commission. 2014. *Co-operatives and Mutuals Commission Wales Report 2014* [Online] Available from http://wales.gov.uk/docs/det/publications/140221coopreporten.pdf?lang=en [Accessed 27/10/14].

Wickham, P.A. 2006. *Strategic Entrepreneurship*. Edinburgh: Pearson Education.

Widén-Wulff, G. and Ginman, M. 2004. "Explaining knowledge sharing in organisations through the dimensions of social capital." *Journal of Information Science*, Volume 30(5): 448-458.

Winn, S. and Hay, I. 2009. "Transition from school for youths with a disability: issues and challenges." *Disability and Society*, Volume 24(1), 103-115.

Wrexham County Borough Council. 2014. *North Wales Prison in Wrexham* [Online] Available from: http://www.wrexham.gov.uk/english/business/prison/ [Accessed 21/05/2014].

Wright, E.O. 2010. *Envisioning Real Utopias*. London: Verso.

Wright. E.O. 2013. Transforming Capitalism through Real Utopias. *American Sociological Review*, Volume 20(10): 1-25.

Y

Young, D. and Salamon, L. 2002. "Commercialization, social ventures, and for-profit competition." In *The State of NonProfit America*, ed. L. Salamon. Washington, DC: Brookings Institute Press.

Z

Zaheer, A., Gözubuyuk, R. and Milanov, H. 2010. "It's the Connections: The Network Perspective in Interorganizational Research." *Academy of Management Perspectives*, Volume 24(1): 62-77.

Zimbardo, P.G., Keough, K.A. and Boyd, J.N. 1997. "Present time perspective as a predictor of risky driving." *Personality and Individual Differences*, Volume 23(6): 1007-1023.

Also Available from Glasnevin Publishing

Politics, Participation & Power
Edited by Deiric O'Broin and Mary
Murphy
ISBN-13: 978-1-908689-19-1

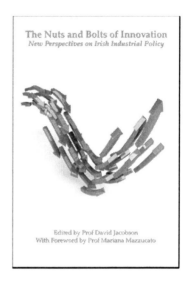

The Nuts and Bolts of Innovation
Edited by David Jacobson
ISBN-13: 978-1908689-25-2

**Awaken the Genius Within: A Guide to
Lifelong Learning Skills**
Samuel A Malone
ISBN-13: 978-1-908689-24-5

Degrees of Nonsense
Edited by Brendan Walsh
ISBN-13: 978-1-9086891-02-3

Lightning Source UK Ltd.
Milton Keynes UK
UKOW02f1536051114

241112UK00001B/1/P